THE
OUTLAWS OF KATHIAWAR
AND
OTHER STUDIES

THE

OUTLAWS OF KATHIAWAR

AND

OTHER STUDIES

C. A. KINCAID

GYAN

Published by

Gyan Publishing House
5, Ansari Road
Daryaganj, New Delhi-110002
Phone: 011-47034999, 9811692060
E-mail: books@gyanbooks.com

Distribution Network
gyanbooks.com
India, USA, Canada, UK, Australia

ISBN: 978-93-7014-587-0 (HB)

First Published, 1905

2nd Impression 2025

Printed at: Gyan Press, Delhi.

THE OUTLAWS OF KATHIAWAR: AND OTHER STUDIES

Author: C. A. KINCAID

THE OUTLAWS OF KATHIAWAR AND OTHER STUDIES.

By

C. A. KINCAID, I.C.S.

BOMBAY:

PRINTED AT THE TIMES PRESS.

1905.

To

The Chiefs and People of

KATHIAWAR

IN GRATEFUL RECOGNITION OF THE SIX

HAPPIEST YEARS OF MY LIFE

SPENT IN THEIR MIDST

THIS VOLUME IS

INSCRIBED.

Nous devons nous frayer nous memes les sentiers par où nous voulons passer,

Et enlever leurs chardons à des campagnes qui n'ont jamais été labourées.

GRÉGOIRE ALEXANDRESCHI.

PREFACE.

In deference to the repeated requests of some of my native friends I have ventured to compile, in book form, the following articles on Kathiawar and kindred subjects.

I should have liked to entirely alter the form of the series on the Outlaws of Kathiawar which were originally moulded to suit the requirements of a daily paper. As official duties prevented me from doing so as fully as I wished, I finally decided to merely reprint them as they first appeared.

I made several attempts, but without success, to obtain a satisfactory photograph, which might serve as a frontispiece, of a thoroughbred Kathi stallion. For without such a photograph I am afraid that it will be difficult to convince my readers of the extraordinary resemblance between the Kathi thoroughbred and the Phidias horse. But if the curiosity of anyone should be sufficiently aroused to make him wish to himself test my statement I can only assure him that the genial Thakor Sahib of Wadhwan will be only too pleased to shew to any visitor his beautiful Kathi horse 'Redo.'

I must, in conclusion, express my thanks to the Editors of the *Times of India* and of *East and West*, with whose permission the ensuing articles are reproduced.

C. A. K.

CONTENTS.

OUTLAWS OF KATHIAWAR.

OUTLAWS OF KATHIAWAR.

CHAPTER I.

THEIR ORIGIN AND HISTORY.

A TRAVELLER by the train from Wadhwan to Rajkote, who cares to while away his abundant leisure by observing the landscape, cannot but be struck by the walls that surround every village in sight and by the watch-towers that, as in the Scotch Highlands, enable a sentinel to observe every movement amongst the neighbouring hills and passes. If he cares to enquire he will be given, amongst a number of fanciful or careless answers, the true reason, that the walls and the watch-towers have a common origin in the fear of outlaws. If he pursue his researches further he will learn that during the last century at least three British officers were captured and either held to ransom or murdered, that in the sixties Colonel Keatinge described Kathiawar as the most lawless part of India, that within the last twelve years a British officer was shot when charging an entrenched position, and that only last year a band of outlaws were destroyed by the common exertions of the Chuda Administration and the Agency Police. It will be the object of this and succeeding articles to give an explanation of the causes of the continuous outlawry in Kathiawar and an account of the principal leaders who, like Jack Sheppard and Claude Duval, have, with time, become the central figures of songs and legends.

Perhaps the most important fact in connection with these outlaws is that they fall naturally into three groups, which have really little or no connection with each other. The first group I shall describe as Girasia outlaws, the second group were the Waghir rebels and the third group were ordinary dacoits—chiefly Mianas—such as are known to every province of India. The first group are by the far the most interesting and are closely akin to the outlaws of early English history. It will be remembered that when the Earl of Huntingdon's property was taken away by John's Regency Government, he gathered together his retainers, went into Sherwood forest, and, under the name of Robin Hood, is to this day in England a household word. His primary object was not to commit offences, although he practically did nothing else. His wish was to make the administration of that part of the kingdom impossible. He succeeded and was thus able to recover from the central authority his sequestered lands and title. The Girasia outlaws of the Sourashtra Peninsula acted on exactly the same lines. They were usually, although by no means always—for as late as 1902 the Judicial Assistant convicted a band of Mahomedans who had gone out against Junagadh—Kathi landholders who had been turned out of their villages by more powerful neighbours. They then called out their servants and relatives and ravaged and murdered until they were either exterminated, or until the wrong-doer realised that peace at any price was his only hope of conducting the government of his taluka and reinstated the outlaw in his ancestral lands. Such outlaws were immensely assisted by the sub-division of the peninsula into numerous States and the fact that each State continually threatened to swallow up its subject landowners. They were therefore the more willing to assist a neighbouring squire in his endeavours to get justice. The circumstance, also, that although their acts were both criminal and cruel, their aim was, in the existing condition of the country, the legitimate redress of their grievances, generally inclined in their favour public opinion, which always heard with approval the compliance of a chief with their demands. I have said that the Girasia outlaws were usually Kathis, and it may not, therefore, be out of place to discuss here the origin of this strange and warlike community, which has given the modern name of Kathiawad (the wall-girt land of the Kathis) to the Sourashtra Peninsula.

Although the late Chief of Jasdan, Ala Chela, once received at a Charan's hands a tremendous* rebuke for his assertion that the Kathis were the equal of the Rajputs, it seems certain that the former have been by far the longer time in India. They themselves derive the name Kathi fror Scythian (Skuthos) and were certainly in India in the sixth century B.C. Indeed they appear to have been one of the earliest waves of that flood of invasion which repeatedly overwhelmed India until the Sikh monarchy closed once and for all the northern passes. That the fate of the Kathi

* The famous lines written by the Charan and sung to Ala Chela in open Durbar, I venture to roughly translate as follows :—

By eating rows of pearls, a crow
Can never hope to be a swan ;
A monkey, though erect he go,
Has never yet become a man ;
The dew that glistens on the stone
But mocks the grateful monsoon shower ;
A jackal, gorged with every bone,
Yet vainly apes the lion's power ;
An ass beneath a horse's load
An ass remains, as all may see ;
The Charan's song although it goad
Must yet considered truth to be,
Ala, I write these lines for you,
For vain and empty is your pride ;
Rajput a Kathi never grew
However hard he may have tried !

The point of the first two lines lies in the belief that a swan retains its whiteness by eating pearls.

invaders was less fortunate than that of the Rajputs* was due to their earlier coming. The power of the Aryan conquerors of India was still unbroken, and although the Kathis might force their way into the great peninsula, its spoils were not for them. But at the time of the Rajput invasion nine centuries later, India presented a very different spectacle. It is now certain that the original Aryan invaders were at first white men. The affinity of their speech with European tongues is the usually accepted evidence. But there exists a still stronger testimony. They not only styled themselves the Aryas or noble men (the Aristoi and Kagathoi), but they were also the men of the Warna or colour, and that that colour was white may be gathered from the epithets of black demons with which they liberally supplied the Sudras. Such a distinction would be meaningless unless the difference in colour was so marked that it at once met every eye. Now-a-days the keenest sight could not differentiate be-

* For the Scythian origin of the Rajputs, *vide* Tod's Rajasthan, Vol. I.

tween a lower caste and a Brahmin if dressed alike. Colour, however, could only be retained by rigid rules of marriage, and these appear to have at first been adhered to: for the author of the Mahabharata regrets his own degenerate days, when, as he writes, there has been a mingling of all Warnas. But time brought laxer ideas and race mixture inferior courage. Then three centuries before Christ came the Macedonian invasion, which was certainly the most striking event in Indian history since the coming of the Aryans.

Kathis and others had, although successful in the field, humbly acknowledged the Aryan racial superiority and have ever since been striving to be recognised as Hindus. But in the Macedonians, the Aryans for the first time saw a fairer and prouder nation than themselves and one which turned away in scorn from Indian religions and Indian wives. Had the Greek conquerors chosen to become Indians, the descendants of Seleucus or Antipator might now be sitting on the throne of

Ramchandra. But the Macedonians would take nothing from the Brahmin. In the double pride of colour and of Hellenism, they refused to "Medise," and after twenty-two centuries the Brahmin has neither forgotten nor forgiven. When six hundred years later another Scythian storm swept over the Himalayas, the Aryan welcomed the invaders. The Greco-Bactrian Kingdoms went down like a house of cards and the Brahmin set himself to weave interminable genealogies connecting the Rajput with the Kshatri. To-day a Scythian sits on the throne of Udaipur and the Indian languages contain no more bitter epithet for the foreigner than "Yavan"—the uncouth and contemptuous Macedonian. The Kathis, however, came at last into their Kingdom. For nearly 2,000 years a wandering tribe, they in 1400 A.D. entered Kathiawar from Cutch and seized Than and Chotila from the Sodha Parmars. At first mere robbers, they after many struggles established themselves at the break-up of the Mogul empire firmly in the centre of the province. They were, however, like the Sikhs before the time of Ranjitsing, a loosely knit confederacy, and they were unable in the 18th century to make headway against the growing power of Junagadh. Then it was that many of the smaller landholders wrote over part of their lands to the surrounding administrations in order to secure protection for the remainder. But this promised protection was not always obtained. It often happened that when the protecting State had acquired part of the Kathis' land, it hungered for the remainder. It would then provoke quarrels, and on some pretext or other violate its agreement. It was useless for the Kathi to seek redress in the State's own Courts, so, calling together his servants and relatives, and placing his wife and children in some friendly shelter, he would turn his back on the homestead where his family had lived for centuries, and, making the Gir his Sherwood forest, proceed to rob and murder in every direction until death, treachery, or redress closed his picturesque but baneful career.

The second group were rather rebels than outlaws. They were the Waghirs of Okhamandal on the north-western promontory of Kathiawar. They had always been a turbulent class, and in early times had been the most daring pirates in the Arabian seas. They are partly Hindu and partly Mussalman, and difference of religion forms curiously enough no bar to intermarriage. They were first heard of in Anglo-Indian history, when in 1804 they plundered a vessel from Bombay. The cause, however, of all the later trouble was the readdition in 1817 of Okhamandal by the British Government to the Gaekwar. The distance of Okhamandal from Baroda rendered it impossible for the latter administration to properly govern it. Three years later the Gaekwar had to call in a British force under Colonel Stanhope to storm Dwarka. The Waghirs then remained quiet until the Mutiny, when they not only drove out the Maratha Governor, but actually led an armed force into British Kathiawar. They were defeated by Colonel

Honner in 1859, and it seemed that the last had been heard of them. As a matter of fact the worst storm was yet to come. In 1862 the renowned Mulu Manik with other Waghirs broke out from the Reva Kantha jail, and it took six years and the lives of two British officers to again restore peace in the unhappy province.

The third group would be the least interesting were it not that the gang-robbers of Kathiawar have usually been composed of a Sindhi fishing tribe called Mianas. Originally settlers in Cutch, Morji, Chief of Malia, in an evil hour for his descendants invited them over to help him against the aggressions of Morvi. From that moment they have been the curse of Malia and indeed of all Kathiawar. The story goes that one day in Baroda a Miana passed an Arab at prayers and asked him what he feared that he should pray. The Arab replied that he only feared God. The Miana retorted that he should come to Malia, for even God they did not fear there. Bands of this tribe have repeatedly gone into outlawry and have even baffled the efforts of regular troops. One of the most troublesome bands was destroyed in 1892, when Lieutenant Gordon was killed. Another famous band, led by Juma Gand, was destroyed in 1894 by the present Superintendent of Agency Police, and, as I have said above, only last year a Miana band was exterminated near Chuda.

But perhaps the most striking figure in this third group was not a Miana at all, but a member of the Atit or religious mendicant caste, and was known by the title of Bava Devgar. I have not been able to ascertain what drove him first into outlawry, but in 1898, when I first heard his name, he had been a dacoit some six years. He was a man of ability and enterprise and probably tired of the saffron robe of the beggar ; and eventually, like Mr. Sam Weller in his early days, adopted the course of taking from his neighbours the things that he coveted, to spare them the trouble of refusing him. His greatest feat was undoubtedly the sack of Nawania, a moderate sized Kathi town in Jetpur. He took advantage of a "Jan" or marriage procession in which all the Kathi population had taken part to enter and thoroughly ransack the town. The faces of the wedding guests on their return home may be better imagined than described. It does not seem that he ever organised a band of dacoits, but he kept closely in touch with the disorderly members of the village communities. And the accuracy of his information was no doubt greatly due to his Atit castemen, who in the " bhangava" garb of the anchorite wandered up and down the country, obtaining news by which Devgar was not slow to profit. If a villager had a family quarrel, if his crops or his wife had been forcibly taken away, if a Bania had, in his opinion, wrongfully sold him up, it was not long before on some dark night he would be confronted by the tall, thin figure of the great dacoit, who would introduce himself as the Bawa who had sacked Nawania. The villager's scruples would be artfully overcome by the dazzling hope of a cruel revenge. A night raid would be skilfully planned, the enemy shot, and the villager left to hang while Devgar was " over the border and awa' " loaded with every thing that he could lay his hands on. However, "sa fin fut funeste," as was written of a greater than him. Captured while engaged in a petty robbery, he was betrayed by his associates, and after thirteen years of outlawry was executed early this year at Bhavnagar. By his death no fewer than thirteen cases of dacoity and murder abated from the court of the Agent to the Governor. His life story has been too recent to have yet gathered round it romance, but in subsequent chapters I hope to give some account of the tales and ballads that have been woven round the great dacoits of earlier times.

CHAPTER II.

RANING VALA.

In my last chapter I divided the outlaws of Kathiawar into three groups—the Girasia outlaws, the Waghirs, and the Miana and other dacoits. In the first group were numbered many famous names, including that of Vala Naja, who in one ballad has been compared to the full-maned lion who, thinking the monsoon thunder is a rival's roar, dies of mortification, and Joga Khuman of Ambardi, the leader of a band of restless Kathis, who indeed were properly speaking more rebels than outlaws. Joga Khuman was, however, the hero of quite the finest quatrain that I have yet discovered in my researches. I give the following translation :—

* The stars may fall from Heaven's dome,
The pride of thrones depart ;
Yet valour still will make her home
In Joga Khuman's heart.

But the fame of all others has been eclipsed by the careers of Raning Vala and his still more famous son, Bava Vala, who will be the subject of a later chapter. The tale of how Raning Vala went out into outlawry affords a vivid example of the earlier intrigues of Kathiawar States and of the mistakes into which insufficient knowledge has sometimes led the British administration. The father of Raning Vala had, with other Vala Kathis, established himself in the Gir and from thence had secured the districts of Visavadar and Chelna. In 1782 they all wrote over to Junagadh, to secure its protection, half of their lands and retained for themselves the other half. They were no doubt troublesome neighbours, and in 1794 the Nawab was glad to give his share of Visavadar and Chelna as a marriage portion to the Chief of Bantwa. This led to quarrels, and as the Bantwa Chief

---

See page 15.

* The original is so fine that I cannot but transcribe it.

Dhru Chale Mera dage
Mahipat mele man
Jogo ki jati kare
Khatrivat Khuman.

Readers acquainted with Gujarati must not be surprised if they find the above unintelligible. The Charan "bat" is as different from ordinary Gujarati as the language of border minstrelsy is from English.

was unable to cope with the united Kathis, he dexterously spread among them dissension and placed Vala Raning in possession of the estates of another Kathi called Matra Vala. The latter went into outlawry and joined the Maratha rebel, Mulharrao, and they were too many for Raning Vala. The latter, however, got rid of Mulharrao by treachery, and although at first driven from Dhari was, in the end, with the help of the Gaekwar's Government, firmly reinstated in both his own and Vala Matra's lands. The latter continued an outlaw until his death, when his widow, on behalf of her infant son, Harsur Vala, successfully petitioned Colonel Walker to be restored Vala Matra's lands. Colonel Walker then committed two mistakes. He ejected Raning Vala from Harsur Vala's lands. This was unfair, because Raning Vala had secured them before the British occupation. And, further, being unable to properly distinguish between the rights of both, Colonel Walker handed over to Harsur Vala not only Matra Vala's estate, but Raning's as well. Then Raning "went out," and after some years died, leaving his son, Bava Vala, to prosecute the family claim. Bava Vala, by his capture of Captain Grant in 1820, was able to move the British Government to restore him his father's lands. The Government, however, committed yet another mistake. For it restored to Bava Vala not only Raning's lands but Harsur's as well. Then Harsur "went out," and four years later, to the intense relief of the Agency, made a midnight attack on Bava Vala's village and murdered him and nearly all his followers. Finally the Junagadh Durbar, in a fit of deep and virtuous indignation, confiscated the lands of both parties and retains them still—"beatus possidens."

Raning, although not the popular hero that his son Bava afterwards became, was still the subject of many songs. It appears that when a Girasia went into outlawry, he rose in his own and the public estimation. He assumed the title of king and invested some needy Charan with the somewhat ill-paid post of Court poet. The Charan's duty was to glorify or console the master, and in return received no regular pay, but a ration and a share in the outlaw's spoils. The following is the longest and most ambitious ballad on Raning Vala that I have met with. It contains some fine lines, but is marred by gross exaggeration. To understand it the reader must exercise a little imagination. He must picture to himself a lonely cave in the Girnar hills, lit only by a native lamp and a wood fire. Round the fire are warming themselves Raning and his band, who have returned from the capture of half a dozen Rathor Girasias, and are debating whether they will murder them in revenge for the loss of one of their own members or hold them to ransom. The Charan, who for some months past has probably received no reward, improves the occasion by first flattering the robber chief and then impressing on him the advantages of mercy—advantages of which the Charan no doubt hopes to receive a substantial share. The flattery is as gross as it can be, for it is a far cry from Kathiawar to Kotah and the Kotah chief's connection with the prisoners is national only. Moreover, a ragged band of Kathi outlaws would not have stood for a moment against the fiery onset of Marwar. But Raning's taste was, one may be sure, not over delicate, and he probably but twisted his moustaches and smiled complacently as he heard his renown "expand like the lotus." I have translated the ballad as follows :—

As on some cliff 'twixt earth and skies
A stately castle rears its head ;
So Raning's fame is seen to rise,
Built on the forms of foemen dead.

If Pauar's lord had never been
The churl had forth to battle fared.
He was the glowing flame which, seen,
The brave destroyed, the coward scared.

In press of battle Raning's shout
The Chiefs of Kotah trembling hear ;
The Rathor's line is turned to rout ;
For once the Rajput looks on fear.

No help, although the world was wide,
To Ravan came when Ram arose ;
Ram's sword now hangs by Raning's side
And drinks the blood of Raning's foes.

His eyes have seen the bitter stain
Of tears on every rival's cheek ;
The moon will cease to wax and wane
Ere they again the battle seek.

The earth is with their heart's blood red
  Their helpless babes and widows weep.
The Charan sings 'your foes are dead
  And like the dead your wrath should sleep.'

Pauar was Raning Vala's principal village. The meaning of the second verse, which is rather obscure, must be sought in the common oriental idea that low-caste persons have no business in battle and that they should work the plough or perform other menial occupations. A bloodthirsty warrior like Raning Vala was regarded as a natural corrective to the degeneracy of later times when the outcaste enlisted in the British army or police and dared to cross swords with the Kathi or the Rajput.

The Charan's duty was not always to glorify the outlaw's deeds; he had, as I have indicated, sometimes to act the part of a consoler. Raning Vala was lame of one leg, but whether from birth or from a wound I have not been able to ascertain. And it must have been on some dark and rainy monsoon evening, when the damp was making the injured leg ache, that the Charan sang the following quatrain :—

> If foot and hand had been but filled
> With equal cunning, might the same ;
> Then Raning would have Ravan killed
> And robbed Ramchandra of his fame.

The references to Ravan and Ramchandra in this and in the longer ballad are allusions to the story of the Ramayan, which tells how the hero Ramchandra conquered from Ravan Lanka, or Ceylon, and thereby recovered his wife Sita. But there is a special reason why the Charan so constantly alluded to their names. In my former article I mentioned the desire of Ala Chela to be considered the equal of the Rajput; and this desire is common to all Kathis who envy the Rajput his alleged descent from the Kshatri and themselves claim to be descended from that noble and warlike stock. No more soothing draught, therefore, could have been administered by the wily Charan than a suggestion that Raning was a descendant of Rama, and that under more fortunate circumstances he might have emulated his deeds.

But the Charan did not always confine himself to chanting the outlaw's praises or lightening his despondency. A great latitude was allowed him, and his sacred character protected him from violence. An insufficient share of the spoil, long continued ill-success, or even sheer malice sometimes prompted the Charan to chant a stinging quatrain in his master's presence. Here is a verse that was sung to his very face by the Charan of the great Bava Vala himself, and it must have nearly driven him out of his mind with rage. The Bhan Khachar alluded to was the Girasia of Bhadli, who, although not averse from looting on his own account, was at deadly enmity with Bava Vala and, so far as he was concerned, was on the side of law and order. Bhan was an energetic, enterprising man, who did not look to the Agency for support, but met raid with counter raid, and on one occasion, to use an Americanism, "fairly cleaned out" Bava Vala's live-stock. This is the event alluded to below :—

"Bava, your herds grazed far and wide,
By wood and glade, by pool and fall ;
Bhan Khachar swept the country side
And ate them up, skin, hooves and all."

I find, however, that I am encroaching on the subject-matter of my next chapter—Bava Vala. This is hardly fair. For so great an outlaw deserves the reader's undivided attention.

CHAPTER III.

BAVA VALA.

In my last chapter I gave an account of the outlaw Raning Vala. The subject of the present one will be his still more famous son, Bava Vala. On Raning's death Bava and and his brother Matra succeeded by inheritance to the leadership of their father's band, and for several years ravaged the country on all sides of the Gir, occasionally making daring raids into other parts of the province. The brothers found, however, that they were getting no nearer their real object, which was the recovery of their father's lands confiscated by the Agency and handed over to Harsur Vala. It must have been then that they formed the plan of seizing some European and thereby compelling the Agency to do them what they thought justice. The opportunity came when Captain Grant, an officer of the Indian Navy, lent to the Gaekwar to organise a flotilla against the pirates of the Kathiawar

Coast, was summoned from Baroda to Amreli. The road led through the Gir forest, and there Bava Vala waylaid him and refused to release him until Harsur Vala was ejected, and in his turn became an outlaw. It was a daring act, not only on account of the prestige of the white man, but also because of the forces which the Agency could and did put in motion to hunt down Bava Vala. The latter, however, successfully eluded capture, and at last, as the sole means of saving Captain Grant, the Agency came to terms. The outlaw's act, as might be expected, gave rise to opinions as divergent as those created by the seizure of the "Rechitelni." The following translation embodies in the last verse the Kathis' view of what they have always deemed a glorious feat of arms :—

Amreli fears king Bava's might
  And Dhari sounds the warning bell
E'en Waghir Manek flees at night
  When you approach his citadel.

Where Gomti, fed by rains and tide,
  Rolls past a hundred shrines its flood
You sacked and slaughtered far and wide
  Till every wave foamed red with blood.

The sahib's helm, the sahib's sword
Had ne'er by child of Ind been ta'en
You, Bava, dared, bold jungle lord!
And ransomed back your wide domain.

The Gomti river referred to in the second verse is the sacred tidal river at Dwarka, once the capital of Krishna, the central figure of the Mahabharata. After a life of love and intrigue he fell near Veraval a victim to a Bhil's arrow. The allusion must be to some successful raid on the Waghir lands of Okhamandal. But the interest of the song is in the third verse as showing the reputation Bava Vala acquired by his seizure of the unfortunate Baroda admiral. The latter, on the other hand, has expressed with great force a different opinion of Bava Vala's conduct in a letter quoted in Low's Indian Navy, Vol. I., page 281. I give the following extracts :—

"I was forced to remount my horse and gallop off with the gang, who took me into a large forest called the Gir, where I was kept prisoner on the top of a mountain for two months and fifteen days. . . . I laid amongst the rocks, drenched with rain night and day, with the exception of two nights, when the gang forced me to accompany them, and we stopped in a friendly village. . . . Towards unfriendly villages it was the custom of the band to ride up to the gates and chop off the heads of little boys at play, and then go off laughing at their cursed exploits. When they returned to the encampment after a day's murdering forage, the young Kathis used to boast how many men they had killed. . . . At night the halter of each horse was tied to his master's arm. When the animals heard voices they tugged and the men were up in an instant. . . .

"My sufferings during confinement were almost beyond endurance, and I used to pray in the evening that I might never see another morning. I had my boots on my feet for the first month, not being able to get them off from the constant wet, until I was reduced by sickness. Severe fever with ague and inflamation of liver came on me, and, with exposure to the open air, drove me delirious, so that when I was let go, I was found wandering in the fields at night covered with vermin from head to foot."

We should all probably have used even more vigorous language had a similar captivity befallen us. But even so, I cannot but feel that some excuse may be found for Bava Vala. It is no doubt difficult to defend the practice of lime-cutting at small boys' heads, but outlawry, like war, cannot be carried on with gloved hands. The unfriendly villages had probably given information to the police, and the band wished to make an example of them. The outlaws dared not enter the walls, lest they should be trapped, and they found no one outside except one or two children, whom they killed and rode away. On their return they no doubt magnified their exploits. As regards Captain Grant, Bava Vala was in a dilemma. A duty had been laid on him by his father as sacred as that which Hamilcar laid on Hannibal. Unless he kept Captain Grant prisoner, that duty would never be accomplished. Unacquainted with Europeans, he at first did not realise that the hardships that he and his band bore with indifference were intolerable to an Englishman. When he did, he regarded the prisoner as a nuisance. His miseries often impeded the flight of the band and brought on them the reproaches of the Kathi women of friendly villages. Sometimes in desperation they proposed to kill him and only refrained in the hope that sooner or later the Agency would come to terms.

The following ballad is a curious one. Just as the critics have divided the Iliad into the Achilleia and the Diomedeia, this ballad seems to have been partly written in praise of Khachar Bhan of Bhadli and partly in praise of Bava Vala. It is really, however, a complete whole, and the explanation is interesting. In the previous chapter I mentioned Khachar Bhan, himself no inconsiderable freebooter, as the sworn and successful foe of Bava Vala. I also described how the Charan, if nettled by ill-success or neglect, sometimes sang satire instead of praise. The present ballad is really nothing but a threat that if the master is not in future more liberal, he must no longer expect from the poet the usual fulsome praise, but nasty remarks about Khachar Bhan. A specimen of the latter is to be found in 4th and 5th verses. The song, however, ends in the orthodox way, and the last line consists of a promise to loudly sing the outlaw's praises—if they are properly paid for (to be understood).

If Bava of the double blade
  Should flee from out the battle throng,
The crops would fade, the rains be stayed
  And hushed would be the Charan's song.

Chiefs who would tame the lion's might
  Or chain the ocean's seething tide,
Yet dread your arrows' vengeful flight
  And scatter o'er the jungle side.

A bloody vengeance, all in vain,
  Your rivals plot and weave and scheme.
As wind dispels the Shravan rain,
  So fades the fabric of their dream.

From where behind its loopholed wall,
  The castled towers of Bhadli stand,
Bold Khachar Bhan, alone of all,
  Has dared to meet you hand to hand.

The men who fell to Bava's sword
  Had fear to Death itself denied;
Yet Khachar Bhan, proud Bhadli's lord,
  Unscathed, the outlaw's wrath defied.

The wild bull's roar rings 'cross the banks
Where Hirun's waters foaming fall ;
But louder yet the hostile ranks
Shall hear the Kathis' battle-call.

As through the glade leaps wild the deer
To 'scape the lion's deadly spring
Those ranks shall break in headlong fear
And loud your praise the bards will sing.

The last line was no doubt accompanied by a profound but meaning salaam.

The hint seems to have been acted on, for the next ballad has, for exaggeration and "preciosity," never, I should think, been approached. The "Rishis" alluded to are the seers who for crores of years have by sheer force of will continued to triumph over death. Yudhishta was the eldest of the Pandav brothers, and his name is a synonym for truthfulness. Bhim was the Ajax of the Mahabharata, Arjun its more chivalrous Achilles, and Yudhishta—well not its Odysseus. I have made no attempt to turn the following into verse. It defies a metrical translation.

If the Kathi were to draw back his foot and leave the battle, how could the serpent support the Earth, the sun rise, or Meru (the Hindu Olympus) not tremble?

How could the sea remain within its borders or the winds blow over the Earth? When the Waghasar (Bava Vala) comes into battle the immoveable moves.

If his warriors were through fear of death to retreat from the battle-field,

How could Brahm chant the Vedas or the Rishis concentrate their thoughts?

If Bava Vala were, when the ready foe awaits him, to turn his face homewards,

The word of Yudhishta would be false, and the North Star would cease to be motionless!

To the Hindu the North Star is the emblem of fixity and Bava Vala must indeed have been dear to the gods if his flight from the Gaekwar's "catch 'em alive O's" would have caused the North Star either to move like a comet in gigantic orbits or to wander about aimlessly like a native servant who, although unwilling to admit it, has failed to understand instructions delivered in some new and astonishing variation of his master's "Bombay bat."

The days of the Girasia outlaws are over. In 1873 the establishment of the

Rajasthanik Court gave the Girasias a forum in which to sue the States. It also robbed them, when resorting to violence, of public sympathy, and lastly diverted into the pockets of lawyers all the money which otherwise would have been spent in the purchase of arms and horses. If a Girasia "goes out" now, he has but a short shrift, and he must bitterly regret the "brave days of old" when a Bava Vala or a Khachar Bhan might ride into the Gir at the head of 30 to 40 well armed and admirably mounted swordsmen.

CHAPTER IV.

THE WAGHIRS OF OKHAMANDAL.

IN the first chapter of this series I gave a slight sketch of the early history of the Waghirs. The rise of their leaders, however, to ballad-eminence dates only from A.D. 1857. At that time the leading man of the Waghirs, both in wealth and personal influence, was Jodha Manik. He came, as his name indicates, from the Manik stock that at one time ruled Dwarka and Okhamandal before the Mahrattas, with British assistance, established themselves therein. Like so many of the leading families amongst the lower castes of Hindus, they claim a Kshatri origin. Indeed all Dheds and Chamars pose as originally Kshatris, while the Bhangis divide themselves into six classes, bearing the lofty appellations of Makvana, Parmar, Rathod, Solanki, Vaghela and Dhori. Such alleged ancestry is, it is needless to say, treated with scornful incredulity by their more fortunate brethren; but who can say whether in the tremendous flood of Scythians, Huns, Turks, Yavans, Jutes and of Mongols, and of all the condottieri of Asia, that kept from the 6th century B.C. pouring into India, many a noble, hunted Kshatri, whose towns and wives had fallen to some northern barbarian, may not have found, with the lowly outcastes, an honoured shelter and taught them to trace back their ancestry to the loins of Rama?

The legendary origin of the Manik family is from Hamirji, a cadet of the house of Cutch, who fell in love with a Herol Rajputni living amongst the Waghirs. The first cause of the Waghir discontent was the Gaekwar's interference with their lands and pensions. In 1857 an incipient rising occurred, and after the intervention of the British a peace was patched up. But those were the Mutiny days, and the fear of the British had ceased to be great in outlying parts of India. Hindustani sepoys in the guise of mendicants penetrated every part of the province with strange tales of the massacre of the white garrison and of the lurid sunset of the British Empire. By none were these tales more greedily listened to than by Jodha Manik of Okhamandal. In 1859 he went with a body of leading Waghirs to the house of the Mahratta Subah of Dwarka and claimed a full restoration of lands and pensions. The Subah, nettled by their insolent bearing, sharply bade them go. They salaamed and departed. The same night they broke out into open rebellion. The whole province of Dwarka and the island of Beit fell into their hands. Jodha Manik assumed the title of King of Okhamandal, while the unhappy Subah was forced to leave the fort by squeezing himself through an open latrine. Driven out of Dwarka and then out of the Barda hills by the British troops, Jodha Manik took refuge in the Gir. Unmolested there, he again took heart, and on the early morning of the 8th October, 1860, performed the great feat of his life--the sack of Kodinar.

Kodinar is a large Gaekwari town on the south-western coast of Kathiawar. Of the near presence of Jodha Manik the Mahratta authorities were aware, and shortly before they had sent to Kodinar a strongly-armed reinforcement; but *d'après la manière du pays* they had forgotten to provide them with ammunition for their muskets. They were all overpowered without loss, and the rest of the day was spent by the Waghirs in the agreeable task of looting the Banias' shops and houses. But Jodha Manik was no miser, and when the Banias had been fleeced to the bone, he spent the loot in feasting the neighbouring Brahmins, whose acknowledgment of his Kshatri descent he wished to obtain, and the low-castes whose support he desired. I have unearthed the following ballad which is written in a gay jingling metre, and affords relief after the somewhat wearisome quatrains of the Kathi bards :—

O! Fair Kodinar, she stands on the cursed Mahratta's lands,
(In the heavens there was neither moon nor star !)
They were Waghirs strong and tall and they climbed the loop-holed wall ;
Then was heard the Banias' wail but their tears had no avail,
When the King of Okha looted Kodinar.

Then a mighty feast he made for the twice born and the Dhed,
And the sweet balls they were scattered free and far,
Though each Brahmin ate and ate, yet he emptied not his plate,
When the lord of Gomti looted Kodinar!

And they revelled late and long, and they chanted many a song.
(O his glory there is nothing that can mar!)
And the Bhats for gifts did come and they thumped the kettle drum;
When the prince of Dwarka looted Kodinar.

And he gave with open hand to each maiden in the land
As she sat bedecked within the bridal car.
Though the spoils they scarce could tell not a single Waghir fell;
When Jodha Manik looted Kodinar!

'Lord of Gomti' and 'Prince of Dwarka' are no doubt poetical variants of King of Okhamandal. Like the late lamented Mr. William Nye, Jodha Manik's end was untimely. He was not, it is true, scalped against the custom of nations, but shortly after this exploit, and possibly as a result of his excesses on that occasion, he died of fever in the Gir, leaving the leadership of the rebels to his nephews, Dev and Mulu Manik, then prisoners in the Rewa Kantha jail. All was quiet until September, 1862, when the two brothers broke from the jail and made their way to Okhamandal, where their return was welcomed with something of the enthusiasm that greeted the escape from Elba. For the next five years they robbed and murdered in every taluka of the province, in spite of the presence of large British contingents and the numerous sibandi levies in Porbandar, Jamnagar, and other Native States. In the cold weather of 1867, as Rao Bahadur Popat Velji, an old hero who still lives in Rajkot, described the scene to me, he, at the head of some mounted scouts, discovered the main body of Waghirs. He engaged their attention by desultory skirmishing until he could inform the bulk of the British force under Major Reynolds and the Assistant Political Agents, Hebbert and La Touche. As they came up the Waghirs entrenched themselves on the Macharda Hill in Jamnagar territory. The force was divided into three storming parties, Popat Velji remaining with Captain La Touche. According to the former, Captain La Touche made his attack too soon and silenced his Lieutenant's remonstrance with the remark "Vania thaish man (do not be a bania)." The result was that La Touche's storming party reached the summit first and received the concentrated Waghir fire. La Touche fell mortally wounded in the abdomen. The party, however, made good its footing, and the arrival of the other bodies terminated the discomfiture of the Waghirs. Captain Hebbert then came up, spoke to La Touche and went after the retreating Waghirs. Night fell, but he did not return, and eventually a search party found him lying shot through the heart. It was supposed that he had received the bullet while trying to cut down a fugitive rebel. Amongst the Waghirs slain was Dev Manik, and the Charan has sung his death as follows :—

> "On Macharda Hill the goddess (Kali) came to drink the blood of men.
>
> "And the Apsuras came in haste to wed the hero Dev (Manik)."

Mulu had escaped with a few followers, but he did not long survive his brother. He was surprised and was shot the following May by the Porbandar police. His name, however, was not forgotten by the Charans. Here is a quatrain that was supposed to have been chanted as the storming party came up, and from its spirit might have been sung on "the banks of the proud Eurotas:—"

Hear the brothers Manik say,
Fame or death be ours to-day.
Captives we shall never be,
Death may find but find us free.

The last line in the following ballad on Mulu Manik will probably amuse the English reader. In it he will find a reference to himself :—

The Mahratta may charge like the set of the tide,
He fears not who often the battle has tried.
They dread him at Dhari, though Dhari be far,
And they shake at his name in remote Kodinar.
The lords of the land may sit perched on a throne;

But he takes all their treasure and towns for his own.
And their insolence fades and their whiskers uncurl,
When they see the gay banner of Manik unfurl!
Awaiting the feast each Kathi reclines,
Mulu comes; at his ease off their dinner he dines.
Deep vengeance they plan. What recks Mulu the bold?
Kings grovel before him whene'er they are told.
And the Rajput and Kathi they fear him the same,
And the white man grows whiter on hearing his name!

After Mulu's death the Waghirs gave up as a bad job their designs on the sovereignty of Okhamandal, and, let us trust, the white man resumed and still retains his normal colour.

CHAPTER V.

THE MIANAS OF MALIA.

I HAVE now come to the last group of outlaws and the only one that really still deserves the name. They were originally a fishing tribe in Sind where their brethren may still be found earning their livelihood by fishing, snaring duck and coot, and acting as beaters to district officers of sporting tastes; and in former days I have often availed myself of their services on the wide lakes formed in the talukas of Mehar and Larkana by the Indus, as in July and August it rolls down in a vast flood the melted snows of the Himalayas. From Sind the Mianas emigrated to Cutch, where they obtained service as mercenaries. But some 200 years ago Morji, the first chief of Malia, invited over to his aid a large body of them and thereby secured for himself independence from Morvi and for his successors endless trouble and humiliation.

It has been said that in high politics no mistake goes unpunished and certainly that committed by Morji has met with its reward, for the present chief of Malia's deposition was due to his difficulties with the descendants of the men whom early in the 18th century his own ancestor summoned from Cutch.

In appearance the Mianas closely resemble the Sindhis, but they have in morals greatly deteriorated from the standard observed in their former home. The women are pretty and frail and no Miana is deemed to have vindicated his manhood until he has brought to a successful conclusion an *affaire du cœur* with the wife of a neighbour. As he has no delicacy in concealing his success, murders and nose-cutting have been more frequent in Malia than a humane Government likes. The Mianas have, derived probably from a strong admixture of Beluchi blood, a very keen sense of humour and the jolly headmen must have roared with laughter when they drew up and signed for the Agency the following recognizance bond: "The Holi being a Hindu festival, in the excitement of which we have no right to participate, we promise not to indulge for the future in our habit of committing burglaries at that season. We promise also to give up hanging about the town gates in the morning and evening and annoying Hindu females by indecent observations. We admit that it is very wrong to make holes in the fort walls instead of going out by the gate. We will not again so offend." It is perhaps unnecessary to add that this promise was, like the fort walls, chiefly honoured in the breach.

I mentioned in my first chapter that as recently as 1903 a band of Mianas were destroyed in Chuda by the combined efforts of the State administration and the Agency police. It was however a sporadic outbreak, for the Mianas' day is practically over. They have been declared to be a criminal tribe, and the Agency watches them with unceasing vigilance. Before, however, the railway track had fully gripped Kathiawar in its great quadrilateral, the Mianas were one of the plagues of the Administration, and the three great leaders, whose names are still remembered, were Mor Sandhani, Vala Namuri and Jama Gandh. It took but little to drive a Miana into outlawry. He hated the monotony of a cultivator's life and loved to make a preposterous claim to State land. If granted, he sold it and made merry. If refused, he became an outlaw. Once a bahirwatia he exchanged the dress of the Sindhi for that of the Baluchi. He let his hair flow unrestrained over his column-like neck. His belt could scarcely bear the weight of knives and daggers stuck within its folds, and across his back he strapped the heavy broad sword that to this day one may see hanging from the wide shoulders of the Chief of the Bhuktis or the Sirdars of Khelat. The Miana outlaw was popular with the Girasias, for not over-scrupulous in their judgment, they gladly welcomed his rollicking laugh and merry tale of successful villainy to brighten the endless tedium of their opium-sodden lives.

The first of the three Miana outlaws Mor Sandhani had some real or fancied grievance against the ruler of Malia, and squared accounts by a most successful career of wickedness. He was banished from the State, and Girdalal, the State Karbhari, fancied that he had gone for ever. The Agency Thandar Chotalal, however, learnt that although Mor Sandhani had been for a year in exile, his wife in Malia was *enceinte*. He went to her house and from her discovered that Mor had paid her several secret visits. The Thandar informed Girdalal, who also saw the lady, but believing in the efficacy of his own police arrangements, coarsely suggested to her that she had found another husband nearer home. She was furious, and on Mor's next appearance made him promise that he would raise the laugh against Girdalal as loudly as he had raised it against her. Mor did not long delay. He and his band hid themselves in a field of tall millet by which the main road ran. As expected, the Karbhari drove past. The carriage was stopped, the unfortunate occupant dragged into the crops, and there, in spite of threats and entreaties, his nose was dexterously removed. Mor's wife was fully satisfied, for the Charans sang her wrongs and her vengeance in every petty

Court in Kathiawar. There must be over a hundred ballads dealing with this theme. One specimen will suffice. It contains two delightful conceits. The first occurs in the first line of the second verse, and I have not been able to properly render it into English. In the original there is a pun on the word "chota" which means Mr. Chotalal as well as little. The suggestion is that Mr. Girdalal's naturally fine manners were contaminated by associating with an Agency official. The second conceit occurs in the last verse. The usual sign of submission in an Indian is to take in his mouth a handful of grass and *ghas khaie gyo* is a colloquialism equivalent to our 'he has been given beans.' The idea is that so many of Mor Sandhani's enemies, led no doubt by the Political Agent, had in this way begged for mercy that there was a hay famine. So the starving cows galloped to Indra, the god of rain, to beg for more grass.

As reckless as Jagdev, the Parmar of life,
With Malia's high chieftain Mor warred to the knife.
Though the Jadavs* are strong, yet he mocked at their might,
Had the gods only dared he had faced them in fight.

---

* The Jadavs are the Jadeja Chiefs of Morvi and Malia.

When the great mix with churls they from greatness descend,
Thus the grandeur of Girdhalal came to an end.
Though the wayfarer loves on ripe millet to gaze
Yet Girdhalal's cheek at the sight is ablaze.

His hand never trembled, his heart never sank,
As Ravan fought Rama, so Mor fought the Frank.
And the cows rushed to Indra their protest to lay
That the foes of Sandhani had left them no hay.

The Parmar Jagdev referred to in the first line was the attendant of King Siddraj of Gujarat. In a bravery competition, he offered to cut off his own head if his rivals would do the same. This amiable offer was declined, and Jagdev was awarded the prize. After six years of outlawry Mor Sandhani surrendered and was tried on several charges of murder and dacoity by the then Judicial Assistant. But as the witnesses in turn met the baleful gaze of the dreaded outlaw, their hearts failed them, for they remembered how on a previous occasion he had subsequently flayed alive a hostile deponent. They could not recollect, they said. They thought the prisoner was like the man whom they saw commit the offence, but they could not swear to him. Mor was acquitted and was bribed to good behaviour by a grant in Jamnagar, were he eventually died, full of years if not of sanctity. The second name that I have given was Vala Namuri. He had originally been a Lieutenant of Mor Sandhani, but had quarrelled with him and had returned to a peaceful life; and it was not until after the latter's surrender that Vala Namuri went out. His fame is derived from the pitched battle that he and his followers fought against Lieutenant Gordon and the Agency police and in which both leaders lost their lives. Gordon heard that Vala Namuri had entrenched himself in a dry river bed and reached the spot as dusk was falling. Fearing that in the night time the band would slip away, he and his sowars charged the position. The young Englishman in full uniform was a ready mark for the dacoits and he fell dead in front of the rifle pit. The police, however, disposed of his murderers, the last one, fortunately, as he was escaping with Gordon's sword. The latter's gallant death made a great impression on the people of Kathiawar and a stately memorial in the Frere Hall at Rajkot bears eloquent testimony that the Chiefs of Kathiawar are not ungrateful. For once the Charan has written a really fine poem and has divided his praise equally between the Miana and the Englishman. I have tried to do to the ballad some justice in the following translation :—

Though the hatred of kings is unsleeping, yet Morvi and Malia were one,
Though they hated they joined for the moment till the days of Namuri were done.

His head never bowed to the mighty, as the wind so his spirit was free,
And he roamed from the Ran to the Bardas, and he robbed from Wadhwan to the sea.

Had Mor and Namuri united, then the earth had been theirs for a prey,
But the love of the lowly lasts always and the love of the great for a day.

Fate's orders, O Vala Namuri, are pitiless ever the same,
Or as stands out some fort on the Bhader so had towered thy castle of fame.

Earth's kings must have kings for their rivals so lion-souled Gordon arose.
Had Gordon not been, then Namuri had robbed from the line to the floes.

From heaven the Apsuras hastened to wed with
the brave who should fall.
Young Gordon died first so they bore him to
wed with the fairest of all.

When two lions lie prone in death-grapple
their pride and their valour are one,
Thus Gordon's fame sprang from Namuri and
Namuri's from Gordon was won.

The last great Miana leader was Jama Gandh. After many escapes he and his six remaining followers were on the 18th April, 1894, brought to bay by Mr. Souter, then in charge of the Drangadhra police, recently re-organised by himself. Like Vala Namuri, Jama Gandh lay in a rifle pit dug out of a disused water-course, and there awaited the attack of the police fully determined to kill the leader and thus acquire a fame equal to Namuri's. Fortunately Mr. Souter, with more prudence, although not less gallantly than Gordon, had discarded his helmet for the sowar's turban, and while the bewildered Mianas looked in vain for the 'topewala,' the police closed with them and destroyed them all. I have only found one ballad on the death of Jama Gandh. It is a wretched piece of doggerel and seems to have been written by a Charan indignant at the outlaw's contempt for his sacred character. As it is amusing, I have made a translation of it. I hope Mr. Souter will forgive me for transcribing it :—

Carts you robbed of every pie
As their way they wended ;
Thus your score of crimes ran high
And you badly ended.

Bania's fat and short of breath,
These you rightly looted.
But you robbed a Charan. Death,
To such sin was suited.

Souter Sahib loved his God
Which was more then you did
So you went beneath the sod
And he hurt eluded.

Brave as Mor was in his day
Quite or very nearly
Souter Sahib made you pay
For your sins right dearly.

CHAPTER VI.

THEIR HORSES.

In my last chapter I concluded the history and legends of the outlaws themselves. In the present one I shall deal with their horses, which really contributed as much as did their riders to the fame which the latter enjoyed.

Classical students will have no difficulty in recalling the frieze of the Parthenon and the horses sculptured thereon. And strangely shaped horses they are, drawn from some equine type now-a-days unknown in Europe. The tapering muzzle, the arched muscular neck, the immense barrel, shoulders and quarters supported by stumpy slender legs, resemble nothing that I have ever seen west of Suez. Indeed the shape of the Parthenon horses I regarded for many years as an insoluble mystery, for if they resembled no living animal then they must have been untrue to their model, and this was opposed to every canon of Hellenic art. But some years ago I was asked by one of the chiefs of this province to enter his stable, as he wished to show me a new Kathi thoroughbred that he had recently purchased. I entered the stable yard and in a minute or so two grooms led out before my wondering eyes a white stallion, the living facsimile of the horses that for two thousand years have so bravely pranced upon the stone whence they were called to life by the chisel of the Athenian. There were the same tapering muzzle, the same powerful barrel showing great endurance, and the same slender legs incapable of bearing a heavily-built rider. Now if—and this will scarcely be denied—the Hellene always copied from life and a living facsimile of the Parthenon horses exists, then the deduction is almost inevitable that the ancestor of the Kathi thoroughbred served as a model to Phidias. But this solution of the riddle seems more difficult to understand than the riddle itself. I venture, although it is the wildest guesswork, to offer the following suggestion. The horses which served as models for the Greek sculptor may have come with Xerxes' Persian army. As a matter of fact the sculptured figures of the riders even appear to me to be too slight for Westerners and are certainly of very much lighter build than the ordinary unmounted Greek statues. May not the cavalry on the Parthenon frieze be Persian cavalry, or rather Greek cavalry equipped in the Persian fashion?

About the Greco-Persian war we know very little, in fact just what Herodotus and Thucydides have chosen to tell us, but even they have admitted the Greek apprehension of the Persian horse and how in the operations before Plataca they successfully cut off the Spartan water-supply and compelled the Greek army to shift their camp.* We also know that after Plataca a large body of Persians under Artabazus escaped unmolested

* V. Grote, Volume IV., p. 267.

and that for many years after their retreat from Southern Greece the Persians occupied fortified ports in Thrace from one of which, Doriskus, they were never expelled. Now in the wide plains of Thrace the Persian cavalry would have far greater opportunities than in Southern Greece, and it is not therefore improbable that the Athenian cavalry, which although non-existent at Plataca took a part in the Peloponnesian war, was organized during the protracted engagements with the Persian outposts. Again, it is one of the peculiarities of military history that troops raised to meet successful branches of the enemy's forces slavishly copy the hostile model. In the Russian war Napoleon, to meet the Cossacks, turned his hussars into lancers. In the Boer war we converted our lancers into Africander carabineers. If the French and English with long historical associations could be so impressed by the advantages of a foreign model, is it to be wondered at that the Greeks who had no traditions should adopt as theirs the Persian system? For the Greeks in their own earlier wars had no cavalry and their very conception of a centaur is a proof that they, like the Peruvian and Mexican enemies of Spain, believed at some not very remote period of their history that a horse and its rider were one and the same animal. A quantity of Persian horses had fallen with other spoil into Greek hands and these no doubt formed the chargers of the Athenian mounted troops and the sires of the later ones.

It will still be asked how Persian cavalry could be mounted on Kathi horses. This presents, however, no insuperable difficulty. In the fifth century (B. C.) the Kathis had not penetrated very far into India, the frontiers of which they had only recently crossed. Moreover the "great kings" possessed an Indian satrapy, and at Arbela part of Darius' cavalry was certainly Scythian or Kathi. Now as Xerxes had the same opportunity as his successor of recruiting his cavalry from his Kathi subjects, it is more than probable that he did so and that that part of his mounted troops which was most effective, and therefore the most likely to serve as a Greek model, was composed of those warlike and skilful horsemen. Moreover, if my guess be correct, it provides an explanation why during the Peloponnesian war the Athenian horse was so ineffective. The Kathi horses could not carry the heavy riders of that day. While the Persian war lasted the Ionian cavalry no doubt kept true to its model. But eventually it was recruited only from the rich and well-fed Attic aristocracy. A two-mile gallop foundered the Eastern chargers groaning under a heavy, armour-covered European and thus it came about that the Athenian mounted troops instead of perpetually harassing the long line of Spartan communications contented themselves with occasionally cutting up a few isolated parties of Morean infantry.

The pursuit of my theory has, I am afraid, led me from the real subject of this article. For the Kathi horse, if he could not carry a heavily equipped Athenian, carried on journeys of astonishing length a Kathi armed only with a sword and a gunnybag for loot. In my article on Bava Wala I quoted from Captain Grant's letter the passage in which he mentioned that while the outlaws slept their mares watched by their side, and on hearing a suspicious sound tugged at their owner's sleeves, and the love of the Kathis for their horses has been a favourite theme of their ballad singers. My first translation deals with Raning Wala's mare Rozdi. I have had to soften down some of the statements of the poet. He would have us believe that her nose was so pointed that she could drink out of a teacup. I have for the benefit of English readers toned down the expression and made her eat out of a goblet. It is not, however, surprising that a horse with such an incomparably aristocratic nose could outpace the wildest monsoon tide that ever thundered up the Balachedi creek or dashed against the temple walls of Somnath Patan.

Like fleecy clouds before the breeze
  The white mare galloped far ;
One day she looked on Dwarka's seas
  The next on Kodinar.

The brave forgot their hard-won fame,
  The great forgot their pride,
When Raning to the battle came
  His matchless mare astride.

When archer's ear met feathered head
  How swift the arrow flew!
So Rozdi to the raiding sped
  When Raning's war-horn blew.

A drinking goblet held her feed,
  White velvet was her skin ;
But slower far than Raning's steed
  The August tides raced in.

As Raning Wala's mare Rozdi was sung by the charans, it was only to be expected that his son Bava Wala's mare Bodli should receive similar honours. The following is my translation of one of the Bodli ballads :—

Now her daily feed was ten pounds of corn
  And two pounds of ghee full-weighed,
And Bava he laughed in merry scorn
  As he rode from each fruitful raid.

She bore her lord from the Ran to the Nal
  From the Nal to the ocean strand ;
Had her labour been spent in pulling the 'Hal'†
  She had ploughed half Kathi land.

She needed no spur on the battle field
  When she guided the charging line ;
But she tore her way through sword and shield
  Like a warship cleaves the brine.

The village walls might overhang
  The village ditch yawn wide,
But she lowered her haunches then wildly sprang
  And the outlaw rode inside.

And when on her saddle they'd garnered the prey
  With a bound she passed from sight,
And the birds that winged their homeward way
  Scarce matched her noiseless flight.

The later outlaws imitated the Kathis in the names which they gave to their horses. Thus Mor Sandhwani had a mare

† The 'Hal' is the common native plough and the 'Nal' in the same verse is the great lake on the North-Eastern frontier of the province.

called Rozdi and I have discovered a long and pretentious ballad in which he chides her for not saving him. The mare is so goaded by this rebuke that she performs all kinds of impossible feats and brings her rider out of danger. But the ballad lacks verity. The Mianas took their horses like Molière took his bons-mots, either where they found or where they recovered them, and at any rate without asking any question as to their antecedents. The Kathis on the other hand kept, and indeed keep to this day, the genealogy of their horses for several hundred years and with much greater accuracy than their own. The Vaghers of Okhamandal as regards their horses resembled the Mianas rather than the Kathis, but I cannot forbear transcribing a translation of one of the ballads on Mulu Manik's horse Manki.‡ She was killed on the Macharda hill from which Mulu escaped, and the loss of this

‡ The 'a' in Manki is long. The word is therefore pronounced Mānki and not in the same way as the common name for our less fortunate simian cousins.

mare no doubt led a few months later to his surprise and death at the hands of the Porbandar Sibandi.

The tide flowed over rock and sand
  When looting grounds she sought;
The tide but covered half the strand
  When back rich spoil she brought.

The Frank might bring her lord to bay
  With twice two hundred men,
At night she noiseless picked her way
  And bore him home again.

Where Macharda frowns o'er the plain
  How thick the war-bolts sped,
Mulu the Gir might hide again
  But never Manki dead.

The blade along the pen might run
  Her ears were still more fine.
And while she lived, save Manki, none
  First crossed the winning line.

No price had bought that matchless grace
  That dauntless heart within,
She lived unpassed in race and chase
  That Death at last might win.

And now with a sigh of regret over Manki's end and a sigh of relief that to-day we can in perfect safety travel from Lakhtar to Veraval, let us say good-bye to the outlaws of Kathiawar.

A GUJARATI NOVEL.

A GUJARATI NOVEL.*

IT will, I think, be generally admitted that the easiest way to the understanding of a people is by a knowledge of its literature. Unfortunately, official duties give the Anglo-Indian but little time to study, and still less to discover from the mass of tedious rubbish, the few really good modern books of the land in which they live. It is in the hope of inducing a few of my countrymen to read the Gujarati romance entitled "Karan Ghelo" that I have written the succeeding pages. I do not pretend to have made a discovery, as the book is known, at least by name, to every educated Gujarati. But my own experience and the periodically recurring gibes of some Anglo-Indian critics on the low standard of vernacular works,

* "Karan Ghelo," by Mr. Nandashankar Tuljashankar. Messrs. Tripathi & Co., Bombay.

leads me to believe that but few of the Englishmen who serve in this Presidency are aware that in the most vigorous and musical of the tongues of Western India there exists a historical novel in which chivalry and knightly worth are invested with much of Scott's romantic glamour, and wherein camp scenes and battle pieces are depicted with all the fire and fidelity of d'Azeglio.

The hero of the story who gives the book his name is "Karan Ghelo," or the rash, an oriental counterpart of Charles le Téméraire, and the last Rajput King of Anhilwad or Gujarat. The then occupant of the Delhi throne was the famous Alla-ud-din Khilji, who in the year 1296 obtained it by the treacherous massacre of his uncle Jalal-ud-din and of his cousins, the sons of the murdered emperor. Until the reign of this capable prince, the Mahomedan possessions in India never, in spite of occasional raids, extended beyond the Punjab, the United Provinces and parts of Bengal. Indeed, one of the most striking incidents in history is the slowness of the Mussalman advance in India and their cataclysmic spread over Persia, Asia Minor, Africa and Spain. How the ragged messenger of Mahomed invited the victorious Chosroes* to acknowledge his master, then an obscure citizen of Mecca, as the apostle of God, and how, when his letter was contemptuously torn in pieces, the great Arabian prophesied that the Persian Empire would be similarly rent asunder, may be read in the glowing pages of Gibbon. The date of this message is uncertain, but was probably A. D. 622, shortly before the Prophet's flight to Medina. Ten years later the obscure citizen of Mecca had become the monarch of Arabia. Another twenty years saw, as prophesied, the destruction of the Persian Kingdom, enfeebled by the victories of Heraclius. The unfortunate Yezdegird, the last to bear the title of Chosroes, was hunted

* Khosroes, the English form of Khushru, or King of the happy countenance, was, like the title of Cæsar, adopted as a surname by all the successors of Cyrus to honour the founder of the empire. Cyrus' real name was Kaikhushru.

from the Tigris to Holwan and from Holwan to perish miserably in China. Of his three daughters, one was married to Ali's son Husein, one died a captive in the Arabian desert, and the third, flying to Saurashtra, the modern Kathiawar, became the mother of the great Gehlote house of Udaipur that still rules from the throne of Ramchandra.* The success of the Arabs was no less striking in the West. At the peace of A. D. 628, six years after the Hijira, the Emperor Heraclius recovered from the Persians, Asia Minor, Syria and Palestine; yet in the 46th year of the Mahomedan era the army of the Caliph was first seen beneath the walls of Constantinople. Within seventy years Northern Africa from Egypt to Ceuta was governed from Mecca. Fifteen years later the Gothic Monarchy of Spain disappeared, like a house of cards, on the banks of the Guadalquiver, and the wave of Saracen conquest, crossing the Pyrenees, covered Toulouse and Aquitaine, till it at last

* *Vide* chapter iii, Tod's "Rajasthan."

dashed in vain against the iron armour of the Franks. The history of Mahomedan conquest in India is very different. The first plundering expedition, it is true, appeared before Thana in A. D. 637. But not until A. D. 712 did the Government of Mecca seriously consider the conquest of India. The army led into Sind by Mahomed Kasim was at first attended by the usual successes, but the Arab historians, after enlarging on the greatness of the conquests, are discreetly silent as to their permanency. Within twenty years the Arabs had but a bare foothold on the coast, and in the end they entirely disappeared. The ill success of this first expedition gave India peace for over 250 years. The Caliphate had by this time ceased to be Arabian, and had become Turk. One of the Caliph's lieutenants had established himself in the Afghan mountains, and on his death, his son, Mahmud of Ghazni, once more made the jehad against Hindustan. The valour and skill of this great captain were as amply rewarded as those of Mahomed Kasim, and the tombs of his soldiers may still be seen near Verawal, where they fell in the famous sack of Somnath. But history repeated itself; not long after Mahmud's death, all that remained of his Indian conquests was the northern half of the Punjab. The Ghori dynasty succeeded that of Ghazni, and the dynasty of Mahmud Taghlak that of the Khiljis, but after the first vigour of the attack, there was always the same erosion of the conquered provinces, and at the death of Ferozshah, but a few years would once again have seen India entirely under Hindu rule. That this did not happen for three centuries was due to the invasion of Timur the Mongol.

The extraordinary ability of this prince's successors, the like of whom the world has never seen, seemed to effectually crush Hindu dreams of independence. But on the first sign of decay that stubborn race once more awoke. When Aurangzib died, Rajputana, the Punjab and the Deccan had ejected the foreigner, and in little over fifty years the Mongol was the suppliant of the Maratha. In this unceasing struggle against the invader, the foremost part was that played by that bulwark of Hinduism, the great Rajput nation, which once ruled from Delhi to the Deccan. Its cities were stormed and sacked, its wide possessions a hundred times overrun, but back and ever back that unconquerable stock for ten centuries cut its way to the lands of its fathers. Some branches of the race, it is true, were lost for ever in the endless war. But a great part succeeded in withholding from the Mussalmans all but a nominal homage. And even that, save for a few degenerate years, was denied by the invincible pride of Mewar. The empire of the Chohan might become the appanage of the Mongol; Bikaneer and Amber might vie with each other who should give their daughters in unhallowed wedlock to the princes of Delhi. Lovely Chitor* itself—the picture-city on

* Chitor was three times destroyed, once by Alla-ud-din, A.D. 1290, then by Bahadur Sultan of Gujarat, in the reign of Emperor Humayun, and in A.D. 1568, by Akbar. On each occasion the women performed the Johur, that is, burnt themselves alive.

the hill—might thrice disappear amidst the clash of swords and the screams of its burning women, but Udaipur had still desert fastnesses and jungle glades where a Sisodia Chief might live on, ill and hungry, but with honour unstained by the pollution of the Mlechha.*

At the time in which the scene of "Karan Ghelo" is laid, Gujarat, which had been overrun by Mahmud of Ghazni and annexed by Muhammad Ghori, was once again a Hindu principality under the rule of Karan, a Waghela† Rajput. The opening chapters find him celebrating in his capital, Anhilwad-Patan, some twenty miles from the modern Messana, the Dusra festival with due pomp and circumstance. Here is a description of the three princi-

* It is curious to note that the word Mlechha has almost exactly the same origin as the Greek word 'barbaros.' A barbaros or barbarian meant a person who, when addressed by a Hellene, could only in reply make sounds like 'bar' 'bar.' A Mlechha (from the same root as મિશ્ર to mix) was a person, who, when trying to talk to an Aryan, so mixed up his words and constructions as to be utterly unintelligible. The miseries of foreign invasion eventually gave to both words a sinister meaning.

† The Waghelas were a Dholka House and succeeded the original Solankis.

pal personages who were waiting outside his palace to do him honour on this fortunate day :—

"Of all those who sat in the space reserved for the village patels, there was none so stoutly built or of such intelligent appearance as Bhano. He was a Kunbi by caste, and in course of his service as patel, he had received in gift many acres from the King. He had also taken on farm several parganas, and collecting the revenues, paid them to the Treasury. He had seen some threescore years, but in his case the proverb "Sense flies at sixty,"* had not proved true. His body was well nourished, and his intellect, still keen as in youth, had acquired wisdom from long experience. His mind was stored with knowledge about the former relations of Kings and peasants, and the extent and collection of the land taxes of those earlier days."

"On the seat opposite Bhano sat, in a place full of dignity, Jetasha, a Jain

---

* The Gujarati is સાઠી બુદ્ધિ નાઠી.

trader. His trade on land and sea amounted to lakhs of rupees. His shops were in every village. His credit was such that his mere name would make rupees spring up, as if by magic, in the desert. Many foreign harbours knew his ships, and his wealth might be reckoned in lakhs and in crores. Those who would have sought to discover Jetasha's qualities, mind or nature, by examining his face, would have been greatly perplexed. It was hard to detect there ability to make and keep money and to conduct trade. His body was so stout that his relatives were constantly worried with the thought as to how they would carry his corpse when dead. He was so fat that his stomach hung like a sack, and the folds of his flesh were so heavy that if any little thing had got lost in them, it would have remained undiscovered from year to year. The heaviest fold was in the front part of his neck, and when shaving him his barber had barely the strength to lift it."

"There was one amongst the crowd of Nagar gentlemen who seemed especially bright and capable. He was seated on a large and ornamented silver slab. He wore merely a dhotar and a rich Kashmir shawl. On his arms were diamond armlets and bracelets, and on his fingers were diamond, ruby and other shining rings. . . . . His appearance and bearing were such that all who saw him could not but feel that he was a great man, and pay him honour. He was of middle height, and although he could not be called fat was inclined to stoutness. His skin was very fair, his face oval, and his nose and ears shapely. His eyes were quick and sparkling with intellect. He was by caste a Nagar Brahmin and was named Madhav. He was King Karan's chief minister. And he had by sheer ability acquired such influence over the King that the latter did nothing without consulting him. The entire conduct of affairs was in his hands. The King was a mere figurehead, and the real ruler was the minister, and for this reason all honoured him and grovelled before him."

Of these delightful sketches, the last is worth particular notice, for Madhav, the minister, is the villain of the book.

While awaiting the King's arrival we are introduced to the palace.

" The King's residence was in the citadel, and near it stood many other buildings. The chief one was 100 feet high, was built of dark-coloured stone and was square in shape. It was surrounded by a rampart studded with domed octangular towers. Some fifty feet from the ground a terrace ran round the entire building. And from it a view could be had of the whole town. Below the terrace were shapely arches and triumphal pillars. On the outer walls were graceful carvings depicting amongst other subjects the wars of Ram and Ravan, the battles of the Mahabharata and the loves of Krishna. The inner walls were painted in rich and various colours and hung with looking-glasses and broad mirrors. To-day, just before sunrise, the gongs in the King's palace began to boom, the drums to roll and the conches to scream. This signified that the King had risen from his couch. He first went to visit his beloved horses. He then cleansed his teeth and bathed. After his bath he worshipped in the presence of the priests his favourite god Shiva . . . . Lastly he ordered grain to be given to the starving beggars who had gathered there in thousands. When this was done he dressed himself, and, putting on his ornaments, went to the Durbar."

Those who have been present at a Viceroy's or Governor's Durbar will be interested to learn from the following passage that a Durbar in the 13th century differed in few respects from a modern one:--

"The vast hall in which the Durbar was held was wide and beautifully designed, and was surrounded by triumphal pillars of crystal. On the floor were spread deep cushions and over them white sheets. On each side were placed chairs, and near the King's throne were seats for his officials, ranged according to their rank.

The King's throne towered above all the others. The cushion on it was of brocade, and over it was a cover of the richest and most costly Bengal velvet. Near it were the thrones of the Yuvrajas or royal princes, but as King Karan had no sons they were unoccupied. Next to them sat in great state the Chief Minister Madhav. He wore a gold cloth puggree and a coat of brocade, and on his body there was no lack of pearls, diamonds and other jewelled ornaments. Near him were the crowned Thakors and the chiefs of the parganas. And there were even present one or two tributary Kings.

On the other side were ambassadors from Udaipur, Jodhpur and other countries. Next to them sat the Samants or chief military officers, who were ranked according to their commands. Then came the chhatrapatis and nobatvadas, who were entitled to the dignity of an umbrella or drum. In one corner stood soldiers, armed with swords, daggers, knives and shields; doctors, pundits, astrologers and other learned Brahmins. Opposite all these were Bhats,* Charans, painters, riding and dancing masters and magicians. In yet another place were nautch girls clad in costly clothes and jewels, who charmed all by their movements, their gestures and their sparkling eyes. Suddenly the Chobdars, carrying golden maces, stepped forward and cried out: "The King of Kings! The giver of pardons! The dispenser of joys!" From this all in the Durbar knew that the King was coming. Everyone stood up, and in their various ways made obeisance. The call of the Chobdars rose louder and louder, and the whole hall buzzed with excitement until the King sat down upon his throne.

"King Karan was in the very prime of life. He was about 30 years of age,

* *Bhats.* This extraordinary people claim to be sprung from the sweat on Mahadev's brow ("Bhal" the forehead and "alta" born). Their profession was that of bards and genealogists, but their principal claim to fame was their custom of going surety for the performance of engagements entered into by the chiefs. Should one of the latter fail to carry them out, the Bhat committed "traga" or self-immolation, and the guilt of Bhat murder fell on the chief. Bhats were sureties to the engagements entered into by the Kathiawar chiefs with Colonel Walker, and within my own experience a Bhat has killed himself in the garden of a chief who would not pay his debt to a bania in his principal town.

and through constant exercise from childhood had remained muscular and strong. His skin was the colour of wheat. His stature was lofty, his face oval, his nose long and straight. His lips were thin and compressed and gave the idea that he was wayward and stubborn, and that his nature was to carry through at all costs what he had once determined on. This had often led him to do hasty and thoughtless acts and had earned him the nickname of Ghelo or "The Rash." His eyes were oval and slightly red which gave a something of fierceness to his face and inspired the evilly disposed with fear. His was the purest Rajput blood; and his courage was worthy of all praise. His chief faults were two. The first was a hasty and fiery temper, and the second was licentiousness. His forehead was broad and his bushy and continuous eyebrows indicated resolution. He was clad in costly clothes. On his head was a golden turban fastened by a brooch set with diamonds and pearls. His coat was of gold lace and his waist-cloth of Benares work. In his golden scabbard were his jewel-hilted sword and dagger. Round his neck were strings of pearls and diamonds. His lower garments were of brocade, and on one foot was a golden anklet. His shoes were of velvet and covered with golden stars. Peacocks' feathers rose above his head, round which the attendants waved their fans. Such was the state in which King Karan sat enthroned."

After the Durbar the king had many duties to perform. He had to listen to religious lectures, the chants of the Court bards, and in the afternoon led a great procession to sacrifice at a sacred tree outside the town, and on his return paid his homage to the goddess "Gadhechi," who guarded the battlements, on each occasion liberally rewarding the presiding Brahmins.

In the evening the king, instead of retiring to bed after the labours of the day, determined to disguise himself and wander through the town in the manner rendered famous by Haroun al Raschid. This, by a fatality which bears a great resemblance to the motif of a Sophoclean play, led him to meet and fall in love with Madhav's wife, the unconsciously evil genius of the story, and from this meeting followed all the ills that overtook him and his house. Her name was Rupsundari ("of the fair face") and her appearance was as follows:—

"She was in truth of the lotus * class. Her face was like the full moon,† and when over her fair cheek the flush of

* The Hindus divide women into four classes (1) પદ્મીની (padmini of the lotus class. This implies absolute perfection; (2) ચિત્રણી, (chitrani) variegated *i.e.*, with good and bad qualities, but still fair to look on; (3) હસ્તીની of the elephant class, with no beauty of face but with an elephant's walk; (4) શંખિની (shankhini) with no beauty of any kind, and a voice like a temple conch—in fact, to be distinctly avoided. The elephant's walk or roll of the hips is produced by the swing of the foot inwards in order to preserve the balance of the beheda or water pots on the woman's head and is much admired. A Rajput friend of mine once told me that his brother had fallen in love with a girl simply because her hips swung in so wide a circle that she took an hour and a half to walk a mile. The slow advance of this majestic beauty must have been as awe-inspiring as the precession of the equinoxes.

† It must be remembered that the term Mah-surat or moonface refers to the brightness rather than the roundness of the eastern moon.

"She walks in beauty like the night
Of cloudless climes and starry skies."

youth spread, it put to shame the pink of the rose. Her mouth was small and her two lips were like delicate corals. When she softly laughed, her white even teeth shewed like a row of pearls. In her nose was fastened a ring of precious pearls, and when they touched her coral lips they sparkled like drops of dew on the red petals of the lotus. On her cheek was a patch,* and just as the Persian poet Hafiz was willing to give Shiraz and Bokhara for the mole on a girl's face, so the kingdom of Gujarat would have been but little to offer for the patch on Rupsundari's cheek. Her eyes were long and naturally † dark, but the slightly blackened lids added to their charm. They were soft and tender, yet they sparkled so that their glance had but to fall on a man to wound him to the heart. Her eyebrows were delicate and shaped

* I have translated *chhundnu*(છુંદણું) as patch. It is really a tattoo mark on the cheek.

† The cosmetic used for darkening lids is called કાજળ and is prepared from lampblack.

like the rainbow, and Madandev* might have used them as bows with which to pierce the hearts of thousands. The chanllo † on her forehead seemed like a drop of blood upon a snowy plain. Her headdress was as dark and shapely as a cobra's hood, and had the hair confined within the knot been released, it would have reached her waist. Her limbs, too, seemed as if they had been fashioned as samples of God's perfect workmanship. Who could resist the charms of such beauty? Man is but man after all."

King Karan, more than other mortals, was exposed to the attack of charms such as these, and almost fainted at the sight. He, however, managed to find his way home, and learning who Rupsundari was,

---

* Madandev, the Hindu Cupid, is always represented as armed with a bow fashioned from a woman's eyebrow.

† The chanllo (ચાંલ્લો) or round spot on the forehead is usually translated as "caste mark." It has, however, nothing to do with caste. It is a purely religious sign. The red and white chanllo denotes usually a Shivaite, although the Vaishnavas and Jains use red chanllos on ceremonial occasions. The saffron chanllo marks the Jain. The Tilak is the oval mark of the Vaishnava. But the parallel yellow lines on the Shivaite are also called the Tilak and represent the crescent moon of Shiva.

prepared, utterly reckless of consequences, to possess her. Next day, on the pretext of urgent business in a distant village, he got rid of Madhav. Rupsundari at the time was in her house, anxious at the warning omens that were continually recurring—here too the resemblance to the Greek drama is noteworthy. She had seen when she awoke a broom standing in the corner. As she came down the stairs a cat ran past her; and when she looked out of the window, her first glance fell on a widow. As she was trying to explain away their meaning, her servants ran in to say that a body of troops were forcing their way into the house. She called her brother-in-law Keshav, who with such servants as he could collect, tried in vain to oppose their entrance. Keshav was cut down and Rupsundari carried off to the King's palace where she was left in Karan's arms. But now other unforeseen events happened. Keshav was married and on his death, his high-spirited widow

Gunsundari determined to become Sati.* Amidst all the pomp and honour to which a Sati is entitled, Gunsundari was conveyed with her husband's corpse to the burning ground. On the way she was accosted by King Karan, disguised as a poorly clad Rajput. He had heard of the terrible consequences of his action, and, hoping to avert punishment therefrom, attempted to trick the Sati into giving him her blessing. But she pierced the disguise, and, furious at her husband's death, included the city and its wicked king in a fearful curse.

"May he end his days a wanderer in the desert; may his wife be led away by the stranger; may his daughter, after endless hardships, fall into the hands of the barbarian; may his enemies make his palace their dwelling place; may his subjects be involved in the fate of the king,

* Sati is derived from સત (Sat) truth, and implies that the widow has adopted the true course. Her self-immolation relieves her husband from any future Avatars or incarnations. The place of her death is usually marked by a stone pillar with a hand pointing upwards carved on it.

and may Anhilpur Patan perish for ever; may its wealth be scattered abroad and its commerce torn up by the roots, and may at last the great city disappear utterly without leaving a trace behind!"

As the Sati in virtue of her act can be refused nothing by the gods the reader is prepared for the impending calamity. But there is one more stage before the cup of the King's iniquities is filled, and that is the suicide of a Bhat. An English reader will probably think this an anti-climax, but that is because it is difficult for him to grasp the terrible sanctity of this strange tribe. The Bhat had become surety for a profligate Bania who had borrowed from Jetashah Rs. 2,000. When the interest and capital had amounted to Rs. 4,000, the banker failing to get anything from the Bania, sued the Bhat. He paid in full and sought his remedy from the principal debtor. His methods were not, however, those of the Civil Courts. He first starved himself for three days in front of the Bania's house. He then brought in turn his mother and his only son, and butchering them at the Bania's feet, sprinkled him all over with their blood. As a last resource he appealed to the King, who slighted him. His supreme remedy had failed, so he stabbed himself in the King's presence, laying on him the awful guilt of "Bhat hatya" or Bhat murder. The cup was now overflowing, and as the last breath left the Bhat's body, a panting messenger ran up and told the King that the Delhi armies had crossed his frontier.

To ascertain how this bolt fell from the blue we must return to Madhav, whom we left, on the day of his wife's abduction, in a distant village. On his return he found his house in mourning, his wife gone and his brother and sister-in-law dead. He could no longer be chief minister. His summer friends deserted him. He could only leave the town. Thirsting for vengeance he went to a temple in Sidhpur, and the same evening in a dream, the goddess Bhawani—the special goddess of the Sati—appeared to him in the guise of a Mahomedan woman, and pointed to Delhi as the path to his desire. Madhav and his friend Motisha made their way to Delhi, and after numerous adventures vividly told, arrived there, shortly before the birthday of Alla-ud-din's eldest son Prince Khijarkhan. Pausing a moment to let us gaze at the crowd of sannyasis* and yogis,

* *Sannyasi* (from સમ્ and ન્યાસ) means a person who has entirely put away the things of this world and is the term applied to the 4th stage of a Hindu householder's life. After the third stage of preparation he must on a lucky day don the yellow garment of the ascetic, and renouncing all ties, live in an appointed place until death releases him. His possessions must not exceed (1) a bamboo staff of seven knots ; (2) a gourd ; (3) a black buck's skin ; (4) a few handfuls of rice made specially ill-tasting to prevent any gratification of the palate. His wealth must be devoted to the building of dharmashalas, temples and wells, and his food must be entirely procured by mendicancy. The *yogi* means literally the man of science from યોગ. But it has the special sense of one who practises the science of mortification. By this means he acquires all powers, even that of living crores of years. Here is a Sanskrit verse describing a Rishi or seer who had done so.

"The lower half of his body was covered up with ant hills. Round his chest was a serpent's slough, while creepers formed a necklace round his throat. His knotted hair fell on his shoulders and the birds nested in the tangles. In such guise and with face towards the sun the seer sat immovable."

The *Veragi* is one who is without attachment (રાગ) *i.e.*, of attachment to the earth. There is another division of ascetics into ભોગી and ત્યાગી (bhogi and tyagi). The latter includes those who have become beggars in a true spirit of renunciation. The former comprises those who did so to shirk work and enjoy themselves. I am told that in this kaliyuga, or degenerate age, the bhogis are by far the more common !

who had gathered to do honour to the goddess Kali, the author takes us to the Court of Alla-ud-din Khilji, one of the most capable and bloodthirsty tyrants who ever sat on a throne. Mr. Nandashankar has here freely borrowed from the Persian historian, Bairani. The trampling to death of the few survivors of a Mongol army which had entered India scores of thousands strong, and the famous scene between the Emperor and the Kazi are almost literally transcribed. The Emperor in open Durbar questioned the Kazi whether his acts in peace and war—his treatment of corrupt revenue officers, rebellious sirdars and his payment of the troops—were according to the strict letter of the Musulman law. The Kazi in spite of the great fear of Alla-ud-din that lay on all India, boldly told him that his acts were quite contrary to the laws of the Prophet. All expected a fearful vengeance. But the Emperor, if he knew little else, knew a brave man when he saw one, and honoured the Kazi with a robe and a present, merely observing that it was not possible to rule Hindustan a day in the way suggested by the Kazi. Into this Court a lucky accident enabled Madhav to enter. In the evening of the Shahzada's birthday a great procession to terminate in a firework display had been arranged. The disorderly line of elephants, horses and camels, covered with jewels torn from all the provinces of Hindustan, were threading their way through the streets, when a rocket, prematurely exploding, set fire to a cart full of fireworks. The most awful confusion ensued.

"The crowds fought and struggled, and those who had knives or daggers tried to cut their way into the open, but were hemmed in by the living fortress round them. Screams of pain from hurts and bruises rose from the crowd. Old men, weaklings and boys were rolled in the dust and with their cries mingled the explosions of squibs, crackers and rockets until the place seemed to be a battle-field. The scared horses and maddened elephants rushed and sprang wildly amongst the mob.

"Rich and poor, young and old, master and servant, pauper and prince were all alike rolled and trampled in the mud. Those who at night slept on wadded mattresses, whose servants soothed and fanned them to rest, who had never even felt the breath of the hot wind, were now lying at full length and their bodies were so crushed that for the rest of their lives they never again needed a shampooer.*"

The young prince was all this while sitting helplessly on his elephant, which had thrown its mahout and was rushing wildly about with a blazing howdah. The prince was in a dilemma. If he remained on the elephant he would certainly be burnt to death. If he jumped off he would be trampled under the feet of the crowd. From this real danger Madhav Karan's late minister, rescued him. He sprang on the howdah, and seizing the boy, jumped

* The point of this sardonic joke lies in the fact that ચાંપવું means both to squeeze and to shampoo.

down on the mob, and with great good fortune succeeded in carrying him to a place of safety. The grateful Shahzada told him to name his reward, and Madhav asked for and was next day granted an audience with the Emperor. There he laid his case before the Refuge of the World,† who promised him to conquer Gujarat and to reinstate him as chief minister under the Delhi vizier.

It was in execution of this promise that a great force under Alla-ud-din's general, Alif Khan, invaded Anhilwad. On hearing of the invasion there were two courses open to King Karan. The course suggested by his leading captains was highly commendable. They advised no active opposition of the invading army, but a stubborn defence of Anhilwad-Patan, while the bulk of the army cut the Musalman communications and gradually collected enough troops to enable them to meet the enemy in the

† Jehanpanah. The Musulman Emperors were fond of compound names of which Jehan formed a part, such as Jehangir (World-seizer), Jehansoz (World-burner.)

open with some chance of success. But the curse of the Sati had to be fulfilled. King Karan, who may be described in Carlyle's words as "without fear of death and without knowledge of war," declared with characteristic imprudence that this course was unworthy of a Rajput King, and that no matter what the odds were, he would meet the barbarians in the open battle-field. The speech was well calculated to dissipate the little caution that is ever to be found in Rajput character, and the small defending force met Alif Khan's army in a strong position not far from the city. The advantage of the ground enabled the Hindus to hold their own throughout the first day, and at night a truce was called and hostilities were suspended until sunrise on the following morning. The Rajputs might have known that the treachery of an Afghan is a byword, but they slept on in perfect confidence until, shortly before dawn, their camp was rushed and their entire force cut to pieces. King Karan was borne away sorely wounded from the field. Anhilwad-Patan opened its gates and the Mahomedans arrived just in time to prevent the queens from burning themselves in their palace. The Patrani or head Queen, Koularani, after a desperate attempt to reach her father's home in Jhalawad, was overtaken and sent as a present to Alla-ud-din, whose favourite wife she rapidly became.

The first part of the Sati's curse was thus fulfilled. Karan lost his capital and his kingdom, and his wives fell into the hands of the outlander.

Some years after the fall of Anhilwad-Patan we are once more introduced to Karan, this time a fugitive living in a fort called Baglan, in the territory of the Mahratta King Ramdev, of Deogadh. We also learn that when Koularani made her desperate efforts to reach her father's house, her two little girls, Kanakdevi and Devaldevi, were entrusted to a servant who tried to take them in disguise to Jhalawad. On the way he learnt that King Karan had been given shelter in Baglan and was recovering from his wounds. He turned south and at last handed them in safety to their father. In five years the eldest died, and four years later, when we are re-introduced to King Karan, the younger is thirteen years old. A tiger hunt in the neighbourhood of Baglan is the beginning of the very slender lovetale of the book. In the hunt King Ramdev's two sons took an active part, and the elder, Shankaldev, saved the life of Devaldevi. Protector and protected fell violently in love with each other, and on Shankaldev's return to Deogadh, Ramdev, on his son's behalf, asked for the hand of Devaldevi. But Karan was a Waghela Rajput, and Ramdev only a Mahratta, and Karan, fallen as he was, held himself immeasurably the superior, and drove out the messenger with ignominy. But news came which made King Karan bitterly regret his pride. His former Queen Koularani had been kept informed of her daughter's fate, and she longed to see her still surviving

Devaldevi. With Alla-ud-din she was all-powerful, and seized the chance of an expedition against Ramdev to ask that Devaldevi might be torn from her father and brought to Delhi. The Emperor readily assented. Alif Khan was ordered to advance on Baglan from Gujarat, while a second army under Malak Kafur dealt with Deogadh. Then King Karan, in bitterness of spirit, was glad enough to accept Shankaldev as son-in-law. But it was too late. In vain Karan called on his old Rajput soldiers of Gujarat to help him. With the few who answered his call and the aid of King Ramdev's younger son, Bhimdev, he held for a time the approaches to Baglan, but a timely reinforcement enabled Alif Khan to carry the passes and blockade the town. Famine led the inhabitants to open the gates, and King Karan thought that the end had come. But one more chance was given him. Profiting by the confusion of Alif Khan's entry into the town, he, Bhimdev, Devaldevi, and the bulk of his troops slipped away and were far on the road to Deogadh before Alif Khan noticed their disappearance. For a time it would seem as if King Karan's troubles were over. But the curse of the Sati had to be fulfilled. Although they avoided the main army of Alif Khan the fugitives fell in with a roving Musalman band, who in spite of inferior numbers, cut to pieces the dispirited Hindus. Devaldevi was led away to Delhi by the barbarian and married to the Shahzada. The author has now only to finish off King Karan. While the pursuit of Devaldevi was being vigorously pressed by Alif Khan, Malik Kafur's army forced its way to Deogadh. But the Mahratta King was no hero. He readily made his peace with the Emperor, tendered a nazarana, and undertook to pay tribute. This so disgusted Karan that in despair he left his shelter and entered on the wandering life foretold by the dying Gunsundari. After a vain attempt to commit suicide, he at last came by his desire and died fighting against the Mlechha. As long as Ramdev lived the promised tribute was readily paid. But on his death his son Shankaldev succeeded, and his bitterness at Devaldevi's loss and his youthful pride prompted him to refuse it. This was the chance that King Karan had longed for. In disguise he sought and obtained a command in Shankaldev's army, and so worked on the prince's vanity that he refused all negotiations. The result was inevitable. The Delhi army reappeared, defeated the Mahrattas and carried away Shankaldev wounded to Delhi. Karan, after performing prodigies of valour, died a soldier's death, and the curse of the Sati was thus carried out to the letter.

So ends a tale that all must read with pleasure. The style is terse and lucid, and free from the turgid inanities which Englishmen, judging from the Anwar-i-Sahaili, often believe to be inevitable in an oriental work. Throughout the book, too, may be found happy aphorism and pointed wit. Mr. Nandashankar evidently kept a special rod for the Brahmin, the priest and the religious mendicant. The 'veragi' who claimed to have attained absorption in the deity (લય) yet disturbed the whole temple if he could not get his regular opium; the Brahmins who, although they received every year the same offerings from their flock, always raised piercing lamentations on the avarice and wickedness of the age, and eventually, after preaching a life of renunciation, so fought over the division of the gifts that they nearly shed each other's blood, are delightful touches of sarcasm. But the scene in which Harpal, one of Karan's former vassals, met the wretched Madhav, who after a brief reign had been forced to fly from Gujarat, is perhaps the most impressive. Harpal could find no worse epithet for the treacherous minister than "Aré Nagra!—O you Nagar!" and when it is remembered that Mr. Nandashankar was himself a Nagar, the reader can estimate the force of this tremendous judgment.*

---

* Since the publication of this article in *East and West*, I have learnt that the above paragraph has caused some offence to the Nagar community. I therefore take this opportunity of assuring them that this was never my intention and of expressing my regret that they should have misunderstood me. I was merely quoting the author's words and I never meant to apply them to the Nagars of the present day.

Those who would search the book for a love story will be disappointed. The romance of Devaldevi and Shankaldev is nothing more than a children's fancy, as is indeed inevitable in a land where girls are married at thirteen to husbands chosen for them by their families. The absorbing interest in the book really centres round the terrible figure of the Sati. Her meritorious death makes the gods her playthings. And though we do not again meet her after her death on her husband's pyre, yet we know throughout the book that her malignant spirit is, like some Olympian goddess, moulding events to gratify her inextinguishable anger. It is she who makes King Karan deaf to the advice of his veteran soldiers, who prompts Koularani to ask for Devaldevi and who finally guides into the Deccan the unhappy prince to find a nameless grave beneath the walls of Deogadh.

Although this article has exceeded its intended limits, I cannot take leave of Mr. Nandashankar's great romance without transcribing its closing passage—a passage so full of touching sorrow for the past, so marked with dignified submission to the present, yet so resonant with future hope, as to form a fitting conclusion to this admirable book.

"So died Karan Waghela; the last Rajput King of Gujarat . . . . At his death Gujarat was widowed; she became the spoil of foreign barbarians, and wild outlandish people made her their prey. Mahmud Begra and the other Sultans of Ahmedabad did her much evil and the Mahrattas utterly despoiled her. Thus Gujarat fell upon unhappy days.

"The time of her greatness has passed away, yet here and there may be seen its broken relics. The Rudrawala of Sidhpur, the Sahastrilling lake of Patan, and other mighty works bear witness to those by-gone days and to the former fortunes of the Rajput. But nowadays, those times seem long ago and five hundred and fifty years have passed since the death of Karan Waghela.

The Gujarat of to-day is very different. Who would fancy that the lazy, sodden, weak and shiftless Rajput comes of that old and vigorous stock? It is hard to think, too, that the starving, useless, ignorant Musalman is the offspring of the Musalmans of those old times. And of the Mahrattas barely the name remains. All alike have been subdued by the fair-faced people of the West.* The Bhats, Charans and other retainers of past royalty are scattered over hill-side and jungle. Gujarat is now in English hands, and may it be God's wish that under their foreign rule she may once again become renowned and great, that with the spread of arts and learning this fair country may become the favoured of God, the home of wealth and the abiding place of virtue. Amen."

---

* West પશ્ચિમ means literally the place behind one. The Northerner who took his bearings from the polar star, faced the North and located the East and West on his right and left and the South behind him. The Hindu, however, took his bearings from the rising sun, which he faced in his morning ablutions. The East was then પૂર્વ the place in front of him. The West પશ્ચિમ behind him. The South દક્ષિણ, the place on his right hand, and the North ઉત્તર or the answering place on the other hand. This meaning of દક્ષિણ the right hand survives in દક્ષિણા, a religious gift, *i.e.*, what is given by the right hand.

And to this prayer will, I am sure, readily assent all those who have ever served in either of the sister-kingdoms of Saurashtra or Anhilwad and who have known and loved their fair scenes, their gallant and loyal chiefs, and their friendly and warm-hearted people.

THE PARSIS AND HELLENIC INFLUENCE.

THE PARSIS AND HELLENIC INFLUENCE.

There are two questions, I think, which sooner or later occur inevitably to any Englishman who serves in the Bombay Presidency. (1) How is it that an eastern community like the Parsis came to show such an extraordinary aptitude for cricket and other western athletic sports? (2) How is it that although for 1,200 years resident in Guzerat, they have, while forgetting Zend, never acquired a proper knowledge of Guzerati? The readiest answer that will occur to the first question is that the Parsis were originally a nation of soldiers before they became traders. But although it would be idle to deny the bold and martial spirit that carried the Persians from Babylon to Athens, and from the Oxus to the Don, yet other communities, as originally warlike as the Persians, have not taken to English games.

Moreover, this answer is no reply whatever to the second question. The object of this article will be to establish that the solution of both problems is to be found in the Hellenisation of Persia before the Arab invasion.

It might be thought that the history of the Parsis since their immigration to India might supply another answer, but there is nothing in it that explains either difficulty. In 633 A. D., as is well known, the Khalif Omar boldly declared war against both the Persian and the Greek empires. An army sent under Khalid to invade Irak was at first successful but eventually met with disaster on the field of Marvaha. But the distracted state of Persia prevented the Chosroes Yezdegird from following up his success, and three years later the entire military establishment of the kingdom perished in the three days' battle of Kadesia. The unhappy king raised fresh levies only to see them destroyed at Jalula and Nehavend. The Arabian army overran the great king's dominions as far as the Oxus, and Yezdegird eventually perished either a fugitive in China or a victim to the cupidity of a miller of Merv.

On Yezdegird's death the great bulk of the Persian population accepted the new rulers, and the province of Khorasan distinguished itself by its welcome. In return, the Arabs did not press on them with any great severity the religion of Islam. For a hundred years the inhabitants were allowed to practise without much hindrance their old Mazdean faith. But as time passed, the rulers of Persia forgot the ready submission of Khorasan and remembered only its existing infidelity. The bulk of such inhabitants as would not be converted fled to the island of Hormuz, from which shortly afterwards the first band of emigrants sailed for Div, a small island off the coast of Kathiawar. The wants of a growing population led to a second emigration to Sanjan, a village in the Thana collectorate, where a skilful presentation of their religion as akin to Hinduism induced the reigning monarch, Jadi Rana, to allow the voyagers on certain terms to settle in his dominions.* The conditions included the adoption of the marriage customs and the language of the country, and the assumption by the immigrants' women of the Hindu dress. The men further agreed to no longer carry arms, for the king was struck by and suspected their martial look and carriage. From Sanjan the Parsis spread to Cambay, Thana and Najmandal to which they gave the modern name of Navsari, in memory of a distant town amid the rice fields of Mazanderan.

One might have thought that the Parsis' religion had been sufficiently persecuted, but the Portuguese tried to accomplish what the Arabs had failed to achieve. In the 14th century the Governor of Thana proclaimed that all resident Parsis should become Christians. But the Parsis showed that they had not forgotten the spirit which impelled their ancestors to sacrifice their fatherland rather than their religion. Force was impossible, and the ruse to which they resorted is worth repetition. They begged

* Menant's "Histoire des Parsis."

for a few days' grace during which they secretly removed their property to Kalyan. On the last day of the respite, and to celebrate their approaching conversion to Christianity, the Parsi community invited to a gorgeous banquet all the leading Portuguese officials. And while the latter were revelling in the rich wines and music provided for their delectation, their ingenious hosts followed as rapidly as they could their movable property outside Portuguese limits.

A still more formidable danger threatened the Parsis when the famous Alauddin invaded Guzerat, to impose on the Hindus the faith which the Parsis had hoped that they had for ever left behind them in Persia. The tale runs that when Patan fell before Alafkhan, the Hindu Governor of Sanjan, reminding the Parsis of the old hospitality shown them by King Karan's ancestor, called on them to resist the Musalman invasion. No less than 1,400 Parsis answered the call, and they nobly repaid the former kindness of Jadi Rana by falling to a man on the plains of Guzerat.

Fortunately for the Parsis, India never became wholly Musalman. Each succeeding dynasty crumbled to pieces before it achieved the modern reality of Indian Empire. Thus the small Zoroastrian community struggled on. For several centuries cultivators, farmers and petty traders, they learnt at last the secrets of commerce and of amassing wealth from the English of Bombay.

Now there is nothing in the foregoing history that explains either of the points raised in the first paragraph. On the contrary, one might have expected that the Parsis, attacked by the Mahomedans and persecuted by the Hindus, would have gradually been absorbed into the Guzerati-speaking body. The explanation, therefore, must be sought elsewhere. If one questions the Hindu, he ascribes the Parsi's inability to talk Guzerati to his natural stupidity, but this is absurd, for the latter learns to speak, correctly and fluently, English and French. The wealth, however, and energy of the Parsi merchants have made the

Hindu prejudiced, and nothing pleases the latter more than to tell stories of the discomfiture of Parsi students. The following is a typical one. A Parsi lad, anxious to pass his matriculation but fearing that he would, if he appeared in his national dress, be at once rejected, disguised himself as a Bania, with an enormous chanolo or caste-mark on his forehead. The examiner considered his appearance suspicious and resolved to test it. He asked the boy the feminine of *mor*, a peacock. The proper answer would, of course, be *dhel*, but the guileless youth replied '*mori*,' a drain. Needless to say, he was promptly and ignominiously expelled amidst the inextinguishable laughter of the triumphant Hindus.

It may be said that there have been among the modern Parsis many excellent Guzerati scholars. This I will not deny. But I think it will be conceded that, although not quite so bad a Guzerati linguist as his detractors pretend, the Parsi very rarely speaks Guzerati correctly. I have heard in my court an eminent Parsi barrister's address delivered in English—a foreign language—with a closeness of reasoning and a purity of accent that would have commanded the attention of a Committee of the House of Commons. Yet when some time later the same gentleman spoke to a witness in the vernacular, every Indian sitting in the court smiled and the witness replied that he did not understand English. I was so greatly struck with this incident that I have been at some pains to discover the principal errors into which a Parsi is apt to fall. They appear to be :—

The substitution of certain letters for others, such as ર for ળ or લ. For instance સંભરાવું for સંભળાવું to remember, સાંભરવું for સાંભળવું to hear; similarly ર is substituted for ડ, for instance, પરવું for પડવું to fall, તેરાવવું for તેડાવવું to send for, અરચણ for અડચણ obstacle. Also ન is almost invariably used instead of ણ, as in પ્રમાને for પ્રમાણે, પ્રમાનીક for પ્રમાણીક, and ત and ટ, દ and ડ* are rarely

* The Hindus say that Parsis have to ask each other whether the "d" is the "d" in Dosabbai or the "d" in Dadabhai.

distinguished. Again, all difficult compound letters are avoided, *e.g.* દોસતાર is used for દોસ્તદાર, સ or ચ is used for છ, as સબી for છબી picture, and ચે for છે. Then vowels are wrongly placed, *e.g.*, દાહારો for દહાડો day, હોશે for હશે may be, ભોનુ for ભાણું dish.

Besides these there are many corrupt expressions such as સકારો for વેહેલો early, વરાવડારા elders, સારીકાંની for સારીપેઠે well, but it is impossible for me to give an exhaustive list of them.

These are the leading characteristics of the Parsi's speech, and the first thing that strikes one is that their mistakes are identically the same as are usually committed by Europeans, whether English, Germans or French. Now other Eastern foreigners have had no difficulty in acquiring Hindu languages and Indian pronunciation. Rajputs and Kathis speak as good Guzerati as any one else. Mahomedan invaders, such as Afghans and Turks, never found any difficulty in acquiring the soft 't' and 'd' of the Peninsula. There must, therefore, be some powerful reason that the Parsi has failed were the others have succeeded.

Now from language let us turn to history. In the early part of the 3rd century B.C. we find in Rome a native drama which, if containing Greek allusions, was yet distinctly national. It was written in a metre exclusively Italian, and in the hands of Plautus was not unworthy of the mighty rôle that was being enacted by Rome and the cities of the Latin league. But a few years later, Italian art, drama, poetry and even music had totally disappeared, and in spite of a national movement unequalled in the world's history, or equalled by the modern Japanese alone, in spite of a struggle in which the greatest genius of all time failed in the face of the burning patriotism of Rome to uproot her dominion, her sole poetic production was the uncouth epic of Ennius. That this decay was due to the all-absorbing influence of Hellenism there can be no doubt whatever, for Ennius took his metre and his models direct from Greece. Yet Rome had as yet only come into contact with the Hellenic fringe on the western shores of the Adriatic. The next two hundred years saw still greater contests, civil war and at last a world-empire, yet Rome failed in art to produce anything whatever and in poetry but the feeblest echoes of Homer and Simonides. Roman historians copied laboriously the methods of those of Athens, the rulers of half Europe deemed themselves happy, if they could ape the speeches of men engaged in the administration of half a county, and Roman women could find no better models than the lascivious dresses of Corinthian courtesans. Well might Horace exclaim that Greece had taken captive her savage conqueror. But even he saw only the beginning. When the capital shifted from Rome to Constantinople, the octopus-grip of Hellenism absolutely crushed the empire out of existence. Slowly but surely Latin ceased to be a spoken language, and when Rome abandoned the Eastern Empire for that of Charlemagne, the laws of Justinian were in the Courts of

Byzantium administered only by the aid of Greek translations. Consuls and Emperors had given place to despots and and sebastocrators, and when in the 15th century, the capital was stormed by the Turks, it is probable, that, in the city of Constantine Latin was understood by the Genoese traders alone, and by such clerks as the imperial embassy might employ to translate the Greek of the Roman Emperor into the Latin which, although not spoken, was yet understood by the western barbarians. Now, if the force of Hellenism was such, that it could first blight the growth of Italian art, poetry and music, and eventually squeeze to death its very language and nationality, it may be fairly assumed that it would not be without effect on its Asiatic neighbours. And this assumption is supported by the little knowledge available. It is probable that before Darius' invasion of Attica, the Persians had a lordly contempt for the Greeks. But not very long after the failure of Xerxes' expedition it became the regular practice of the great king to employ Greek mercenaries, and

Xenophon's retreat gives the reader an idea of their numbers. Eventually, the Persian Government became so hypnotised by the fancied superiority of Greek arms that Alexander's conquest of the country was barely more than a *promenade militaire.* After Arbela followed eighty years of Greek rule, and when the effect of Hellenism in subjection has been seen, the effect of Greek domination may be imagined. Had the Seleucidæ not been succeeded by the Parthian Arsaces, it is probable that the Persian tongue would have vanished and that Persia would have even ceased to be a geographical expression. Nearly five hundred years of a purely Asiatic rule did much, no doubt, to stay the progress of Hellenism, but the plant was hard to kill, and when in 226 A.D., Ardeshir founded the dynasty of the Sassanides it began to again flourish exceedingly. Barely 100 years after Ardeshir's revolution, Constantine removed the seat of the Roman Empire to Byzantium, and from that year until Bahram's revolt in A.D. 590 the two empires were almost continually at war.

Now it is doubtful whether this internecine struggle was not one of the most favourable atmospheres for the spread of Greek influence. Greek provinces were continually coming under Persian rule and modifying Persian ideas. On the other hand Persian Satrapies were as often overrun by Greek armies and subjected to Western laws. But Bahram's revolt gave the Greeks a supreme chance of which we may be sure they made the most. The grandson of the great Nushirvan was driven a fugitive from Modain, and it is worthy of note that when this Asiatic prince looked for a refuge he preferred the Court of the Greek Emperor to the alliance of the Scythians or the Turks. The Emperor Maurice gladly supported the royal fugitive, married him to his daughter and never rested until the Chosroes was once more a king and Bahram a fugitive. As the body-guards of the Persian empress, a thousand Greek mercenaries were enlisted, and when the recent influence of an English princess on the Prussian Court is remembered, one can conceive how the presence of this great Greek lady must have affected Persian manners. For the Chosroes was till her death her devoted slave, and the loves of Parviz and Shirin are still the theme of the versifiers of Teheran.

The Emperor Maurice died only thirty years before the Arab invasion, and it is significant that the Government of Mecca, when it declared war, did so upon both Empires at once. This has always been regarded as an instance of unequalled audacity. The better explanation is probably that the Arabs could not help themselves. They knew that the two nations had, in spite of their continual fighting so much in common, that the Persians would, against their fellow Asiatics, inevitably join with the Greeks. Mecca therefore, anticipated events by invading at one time the territories of Persia and Constantinople.

Let us now recapitulate the evidence produced. I have shown from the history of Rome, with what force Hellenism, if given the opportunity, could spread. I have further pointed out the unrivalled opportunity that it obtained in the latter days of the Persian monarchy. I have indicated, perhaps rather out of place, that the mistakes in speaking the vernacular committed by a Parsi are the same as those committed by a European. Again, no Eastern community except the Parsis have after a few generations in the Indian Peninsula been able to preserve their distinctive nationality. Can any one distinguish at a glance a Turk from a Mongol or from a resident Pathan? Is a Mahomedan of foreign descent in any way to be separated from a converted Hindu? Afghans, Mongols, and Turks are alike Indians, and if replaced in Cabul, Mongolia or Turkestan would feel lost in their ancestral surroundings. On the other hand, the Westerner has never failed to preserve his nationality. The Macedonian refused to mix with the Indian population and the Greco-Bactrian coins shew that as long as those monarchies endured, the ruling class remained purely Hellene. An Englishman in India is as much an Englishman as in

London, and a few ounces of European blood have built up the Goanese into a separate nation. Yet, in spite of this hard and fast rule, we find a small Eastern community living in the midst of the most Hindu centres, and yet as distinct a nation as ourselves. It may be said that the Parsi, if deported to Teheran would be as lost as a Mongol in Mongolia. But that is because Persia has changed, and not he. There are still in the wilds of Korasan a Zoroastrian remnant who practise the same religion, use in their prayers the same mystical language, and the same rites as the Parsis of Bombay. With them the Parsis, after seven centuries of exile, renewed and preserved relations and, to their eternal glory, used their great wealth and their vast influence with the British Government to alleviate the lot of their unfortunate brothers who still struggled on beneath the tyranny of the Shah.* Were the modern Parsis to be dumped down in Khorasan,

---

* The diplomatic efforts which in 1882 ended in this happy result cost Sir Dinshaw Petit and the Persian Zoroastrain Amelioration Fund Rs. 1,09,564.

they would soon mingle with their fellow Zoroastrains, although through twelve centuries they have refused to mingle with the Hindus. Further, is not one of the most notable characteristics of the Indian his inability to understand mechanics, and the fatal facility with which he jams any complicated machinery placed in his hands? Yet the Parsi is a born engineer. He works the mills of India from Madras to Cawnpore, and the engines of the coasting steamers from Karachi to Calcutta. Again, although the Deccani Brahmins are undoubtedly developing a certain aptitude for cricket, is not aversion from all except equestrian games a characteristic of the native? Yet the fields and maidans of Bombay are crowded with Parsi cricketers and tennis-players. It appears to me that my theory is the only one that fits with these facts. The Court, the nobles, the merchants of Persia, had after twelve centuries of proximity and intercommunication become as Hellene as the Greeks themselves. It is possible that the lower classes were not so deeply affected, just as in Russia to-day where, while the Slav aristocracy has become thoroughly European, the Moujik has not yet altogether thrown off the East. For the masses, the relapse to an oriental life and religion was no great step. But all that was brightest and most highly bred in the great king's dominions, fled to the mountainous deserts of Khorasan where they hoped, from its inaccessibility and their own professions of loyalty, to escape the pollution of the barbarian.* No doubt the majority had Greek blood in their veins, inherited from Corinthian favourites, or Aetolian mercenaries, and to them the rule of the Arab savage must have been doubly odious. For a hundred years their distant home saved them from interference, but at last the Arab penetrated even there. Then the *elite* of the exiled community sought a refuge on the ocean, and came to India. There their Hellenic ideas prevented them from sinking into one of the submerged

* Barbarian means one who says 'barbar' instead of using the melodious language of Attica.

classes, kept them from even properly learning the languages of the Peninsula, and thus we have the modern Parsi—skilful at mechanics, because the Greeks were the artificers of the Roman Empire, athletic because all athletics date from Olympia, unwilling to learn Guzerati, for does not the word barbarian itself show the Hellenes' contempt for all tongues save that spoken in his own diminutive country? If my conclusions be correct, then surely the modern Parsi is the most fascinating proof of the strength of that Hellenism which for twenty-three centuries has so largely influenced the growth of modern Europe. Here is an Eastern nation, westernised and through twelve centuries kept western, until on contact with the English it throws off the few particles of oriental influence that during that period has adhered to it, and now at last stands revealed by its thoughts, manners, mode of speech and ideals as a western nation living in the very heart of Asia.

THE
STORY OF HARPAL MAKWANA.

THE STORY OF HARPAL MAKWANA.

THE HERO OF JHALAWAD.

The story of Harpal Makwana, the eponymous hero of Jhalawad, has already been told in the Ras Mala, and at greater length by the author of 'Karan Ghelo.' But the tale is one that, in my opinion, will bear retelling, especially as I have fortunately secured a ballad which either escaped the notice of Mr. Forbes and Mr. Nandashanker, or because of an anachronism was rejected by them. Yet if carefully scrutinized it enables the reader to fix the exact time and spot of Harpal's death.

Harpal Makwana was the grandson of King Vahiyas of Karantigadh in Cutch. When the old king was nigh to death he gathered round him his relations, who, standing by his bedside, waited patiently that his soul might obtain release. But King Vahiyas, like King Charles II, was an unconscionable time a-dying. At last his son Kesar asked what troubled his father that he died not. King Vahiyas answered that King Hamir of Samaya was his bitter enemy, and that, unless someone promised him that he would from King Hamir's stables steal 125 horses, death would not come to King Vahiyas. Prince Kesar promised and life left the dying King. When, however, the prince came to fulfil his promise difficulties arose. No one would follow him. But, as the proverb says, "There is no strength like one's own strength and no water like rain water." So Prince Kesar gathered his servants, raided Samaiya and carried back the horses. This dazzling success was, however, the beginning of his misfortunes. For ten or twelve years he did nothing but harry his powerful neighbour's country. Horses, camels, wives were in turn brought in triumph to Karantigadh. At last King Hamir sent a herald and asked for terms. But King Kesar only said "Come and fight." King Hamir objected that he could not in so barren a land support an army. Prince Kesar answered "If you come I will sow for its subsistence 1,000 acres of wheat." So King Hamir came, and he killed every man, woman and child in Karantigadh. He burnt down the houses and beneath them ploughed up the ground. One son alone escaped from the massacre, Harpal the hero of our story. He was first cousin of King Karan Waghela, who then reigned over Gujarat. When he reached Patan, the capital, things were going badly with its ruler. King Karan had carried off, to his own zenana, his diwan's wife, and in the affray the latter's brother Keshav had been killed. To revenge itself Keshav's soul turned into a 'bhut' or evil genii, and entered the body of King Karan's wife, the beautiful Kaularani. Not satisfied with this, the genii amused itself by breaking windows and doing similar mischief. And as Harpal neared Patan, the genii had thrown a maiden into a well. The terrified crowd did nothing, but the Makwana jumped in and pulled her out. Taking this as a good augury he entered

Patan, made full enquiries as to the conduct and identity of the genii, and considering that if he could but cast it out he would be certain of a cordial welcome, took measures to do so. It is here that my ballad, or rather series of ballads—for the poem consists of several parts by different hands—begins. It differs in some measure from the story as given in the 'Karan Ghelo'. There Harpal went to the burning ground merely to test the eficacy of his exorcising charms. In my poem his object is not given, but while there he met the goddess Shakti, an attendant of Ambabhavani, who afterwards became his wife, and was the founder of bis fortunes. She had been searching the earth for a suitable husband, but till then had not found anyone to satisfy her difficult taste. But here I shall let the poet tell his tale through the medium of my translation.

He came where Patan's temple bel
Strikes loud across the plain.
A maid when watering at the well
Missing her footing inwards fell.

The gaping crowd but wailed aloud,
Though shrill the maiden's outcries rang;
Then Harpal to the water sprang,
And drew her forth again.
The Rajput thought that deem he should
For future fame the omen good;
Within the Patan gates he stood
Last left of all his band.
His hopes were high, his courage whole;
He learnt an evil Nagar's soul
For Karan's sins had taken as toll
The queen of Gujarland.
Makwana's fiery spirit burned
For fame and honours hardly earned:
In charms and mantras deeply learned
He sought the burning ground.
'Twas Asho's* last and darkest night,
The ghosts shrieked round the daring wight,
And though from childhood trained to fight
He shuddered at the sound.
Two kids beneath his arms he brought,
Their throats his polished dagger sought,
And as of old the wizards taught
He let the blood flow free.
Then saw before his wondering eyes
The goddess Shakti slowly rise
And swiftly lap the sacrifice.

* The real date was the Kali Chaudish (the Indian All Hallow's eve), *i.e.*, Asho Vad 14 not Asho Vad 15.

To slake the Devi's raging thirst
The victims' blood he offered first ;
She craved for more and came more nigh
He plunged the blade within his thigh.
And where the red blood spouted high
Drank Shakti greedily.
Then glad she blessed the Rajput's quest,
And cried with passions' fire possessed :—
" Be he but proved by one more test
My husband he shall be."

The English reader will probably consider the poet's tale as jerky as Mr. Alfred Jingle's speech. But then he must remember that the Charan addressed his song to an audience who knew from childhood every incident in the story. It was unnecessary to tell them that the genii had pushed into the well the rescued maiden or who Shakti was. The night was short. Other Charans were waiting to sing their songs, so just as Mark Twain had to sacrifice for the King of Prussia's whiskers, his Majesty's epaulettes, the bard abandoned the minor details that he might get on with his story. The second test of which the goddess spoke is related in the second part of the poem. When Harpal was returning home from the burning ground he saw a woman standing alone at the same well from which he had saved the girl. He asked for water. She did not answer. He asked again, but got no reply. Then he plucked her skirt. The woman grew as tall as the clouds. Her nostrils became like mountain caves, and her eyes glared like village tanks in April. From this commanding position Shakti—for it was she—proceeded to deride the baffled Rajput. He, however, struck her a violent blow with his *lathi* and after a tremendous struggle, in the course of which she satisfied herself that she had at last found a suitable husband, she agreed to marry him; but on one condition. If anyone but Harpal learnt her divine nature, she would leave him for ever.

They were duly married, and with her aid and his own science he succeeded in casting out the evil genii. In return Harpal as a reward demanded from King Karan that he should be given as many villages as he could in a single night decorate with garlands. King Karan thought of the bad roads and the distance between the villages, and agreed. But next morning he was horrified to learn that between 9 p.m. and 4 a.m. Harpal, with the aid of Shakti and the now conquered genii, had decorated the town of Patdi and 2,000 other villages. Five hundred of these Harpal was induced by Kaularani to restore, but fifteen hundred he retained. The genii, however, began to be unpleasant, and it threatened to eat up Harpal unless he gave it some work to do. But Shakti was too many for it. At her suggestion Harpal directed it to fix in the ground a bamboo pole and climb up and down it to all eternity—and then come for further orders. What the genii said has not been recorded, but it may be assumed that into its feelings disgust entered largely.

When King Karan Waghela was in 1297 A.D. driven by Alauddin from Gujarat, Harpal first fought in defence of Patan, and then fell back on his fief of Patdi which, no doubt with Shakti's assistance, he successfully defended against the Mahomedans. At Patdi three sons and a daughter were born. One day, when their lives were endangered by a mad elephant, Shakti stretched out her hand and seizing them drew them inside the palace. From that day forth the boys were known as Jhala Rajputs from 'Jhalvun,' the Gujarati verb meaning 'to sieze'. And from them has Eastern Kathiawad derived the name of Jhalawad—the wall-girt land of the Jhalas. But here again I will let the poet tell his own tale.

They lived where Patdi's towers soar,
In happy wedlock children four—
Three boys, a girl—the goddess bore
Unto her bosom's lord.
The princes on a Magsur day,
With Mulu Charan went to play;
Sweet tales he told them by the way
Of Ram and Rama's sword.
An elephant, Gajraj by name,
With winter lust his heart aflame
Had burst his chains and furious came
Where stood the palace ward.

In vain alike was flight or strife;
In vain the sentries gave their life;
The monster's hate and strength and weight
Bore down both horse and man.
The lads still lingered in the street.
They heard the Charan's fabling sweet;
They heeded not Gajraj's feet
That thundered as he ran.
Then Harpal's heart with anger burned,
He drew his sword and swiftly turned,
One moment more the brute had spurned
The princes and their sire.
But on his sword arm Shakti laid
Her hand, and Harpal's going stayed
"Shall I at once be childless made
"And widowed mount the pyre?"
She put her arm the casement through,
Her arm it grew and grew and grew
Until her sons she safely drew
Within the palace room.
But through the town the wonder spread,
One gossip to another said
'Did Harpal then a goddess wed?'
And thus came Harpal's doom.
One morn the goddess Shakti spoke
"They've learned my tale these city folk;
The bond between us now is broke."

Entreaties Harpal vainly spent,
In vain wild prayers to Shiv he sent,
But when was goddess' purpose bent
By prayers of mortal men ?
The princes' tears too flowed in vain,
Her word she ne'er took back again.
One night when roared the Shravan rain
She vanished from their ken.

Mr. Forbes and Mr. Nandashanker, while mentioning the rescue of the children and their subsequent name of Jhalas, neither allude to Shakti's disappearance nor to Harpal's end. It was always repugnant to me that so great a warrior should not have died on the battlefield, and I was delighted when the last part of my poem established that he did so. It is in a different metre from the other parts, and in a lighter strain. I shall first give my translation and then my comments on it

One day when Siddhraj by the Nal
  Right gaily went shikarring;
News came that Hindu and Moghal
  And Parsi all were warring.

They fought so hard, the blood so flowed
God's throne became unsteady,
So Sidhraj up to Harpal rode,
'Makwana, bold, make ready.

'You'll ride to Khambhat in two days—
'My word goes not unheeded—
'And stop the fight.' Brave Harpal says:
'Two days are hardly needed.'

The shields they rang, the swords they played
The wounds as swiftly followed;
And such as met bold Harpal's blade
In dust and gore soon wallowed.

At last he fought the Turks alone
By everyone forsaken;
For all his warriors one by one,
Were wounded, killed or taken.

He sent a sowar for help to call—
King Siddhraj, were you sleeping?—
It never came and Harpal's fall
Sent Kshatridom a weeping.

The first criticism that suggests itself is that Harpal Makwana lived nearly two hundred years after King Siddhraj. But this is, I think, to be answered as follows:—The writer is clearly no historian, and is only recording a tradition that he does not fully understand. He knew that Harpal was a contemporary of King Karan Waghela, and he confounded the latter with his great predecessor, King Karan Solanki. The Charan also knew that Harpal outlived King Karan's fall, and he therefore described Harpal's death as occurring in the reign of King Siddhraj, Karan Solanki's successor. But what was the battle in which Mahomedans, Hindus and Parsis all took part? So far as I know there is only one in history, and that corresponds with the probable date of Harpal's death, who, it may be presumed, did not long survive Shakti's departure. If one turns to Menant's "Histoire des Parsis," page 20, one learns that seven years after the capture of Patan, its conqueror Alif Khan carried his victorious arms as far south as Sanjan. In his despair the ruler of the town, a former feoffee of King Karan, called to his help the Parsis of Gujarat and Cambay. As he did so he reminded them of the shelter given them 500 years before at this very Sanjan by

Jadi Rana (King Vanraj). The Parsis, to their eternal glory, responded nobly to the call, and 1,400 of them, under a leader Ardeshir, tried to raise the siege. They failed and perished to a man. Now in the poem the scene of the battle is Khambat (Cambay) and not Sanjan. But Alif Khan's expedition set forth to conquer Cambay, and only incidentally proceeded further south. The Parsi force, too, came chiefly from Cambay, and thus the poet's error is quite excusable. It is also noticeable that though at first the three parties seem to have fought a three cornered duel, the penultimate verse shows that it was the Turks (the vulgar name for all kinds of Mahomedans) who were Harpal's enemies. The Parsis and Hindus were therefore allies, and I do not think that we shall be wrong in conjecturing that Shakti's husband set out with the relieving army of which Ardeshir's heroic force was the nucleus, and that beneath the walls of the doomed city where the Mleccha dead lay thickest might have been found the mortal remaius of Harpal Kesar.

So lived and died the great Makwana. But his fame continued to inspire through the Charan's verses the gallant stock sprung from his loins and his soul lived on in the great Palatine houses of Dhraugadhra, Wadhwan, Limdi and Lakhtar, that in spite of Mussulman invasion and Maratha intrigue kept for five centuries intact the ancient freedom of Saurashtra.

ENVOI.

ENVOI.

Kathiland.

Would you know the joys of waking ere the earliest dawn is breaking,
Lest the cheetul at the pool should drink his fill?
Would you know the joys of sitting till the night-birds are aflitting,
That the panther may return unto his kill?
You shall know them at Tellala where the Hirun rushes foaming,
As it strives in vain to batter down its weir;
Where the sambhur bells the night through to the hinds that may be roaming,
And the lions wake the echoes of the Gir.

Would you know the joys of driving across English-built sand-bunkers?
Where the grassy links are stretched out true and flat,
While your caddy looks with envy at the cooly on his hunkers,
And marvels what on earth you would be at?

Book your kit for Balachedi 'mid the lone Jamnagar dead-lands,
Where four hundred yards divide the hole and tee,
Where across the silent landscape shimmer Cutch's distant head-lands,
And a golden glory rests upon the sea.

Has your heart ne'er throbbed to breaking while the sounder quits the cover?
And you strive to solve the riddle where they'll make;
While your mare stands like a statue till the squeaker-rush is over,
For she knows the boar is lurking in the brake?
No? Then soon as you are able, write Upleta on your label,
Bring some trusty seasoned hunter that you know,
For the boar will race and bend him and you'll have to spear and end him,
Ere his tushes on your table you may show.

Would you know the endless gallop till the white buck is surrounded,
Or the grey wolf struggles silent on your spear?
Would you know the joy unrivalled when the blue bull staggers wounded,
As the blade is through his barrel driven sheer?

Go to Wadhwan, go to Chuda, where the plain
 rolls on unending,
Where the herds unnumbered graze upon the
 ling,
Where a Waler mare whose rider holds a spear
 point straight beside her,
Is the equal *proved* of any living thing.

Would you serve among a people who will learn
 to like and know you,
Whom you in turn will love and understand;
Where a Talukdar on horseback still a trick or
 two can show you—
The kindly loyal chiefs of Kathiland?
Then make suitable petition to the Sirkar that
 they send you
To this land of river, forest and of field,
And when you are gazetted pray Parmeshvar
 that he lend you
The sight to make its beauties stand revealed.

Yes, Kathiland I love you, right from Bavli to
 Porbunder,
Under any sort of aspect, any skies.
Though best loved by the ocean where the
 league-long rollers thunder
And the blow whale's fitful fountains dimly rise.

I shall love you still hereafter, through the
  years that are to follow,
And wheresoe'er my station be assigned ;
Where the May mists hide the hill tops or the
  June sun grips the hollow,
Where the Indus roars at flood time or the
  thatched eaves house the swallow—
Yet my heart within your borders you will find.

I shall see the pintail preening in the pools along
  the Bhader,
I shall hear the partridge calling from the wheat ?
I shall see the wide Nal dotted with the wild
  duck and the wader,
As the reed-raft bears the gunner to the beat ;
I shall see the pig break cover from the grass
  clump and the thicket,
I shall see the little chink upon the Dhar.
*And ! by Jove ! I'll wire for short leave and I'll buy
  a week-end ticket,*
And I'll take the Friday train to Kathiawar !